Hauntings

Hauntings

BARNES
&NOBLE
BOOKS
NEW YORK

CONTENTS

The Silent Stone Sentinels

Standing in mute witness to the passions and intrigues of generations they have sheltered, certain houses seem to harbor the shades of their own pasts. Along the hallways and battlements of ancient, windswept castles, in the musty gloom of fog-shrouded mansions, old wrongs and evils and longings seem not to die, but to cling like mist to the cold stones that saw their origins.

Legends of haunted houses are age-old. But are ghosts real, or are they merely human inventions conjured from the miasmic air and forboding presence of certain dwellings? Some psychical researchers have suggested that ghosts do haunt houses, if only as nebulous afterimages of particularly strong feelings and portentous events. The physicist Sir Oliver Lodge, for instance, proposed in 1908 that hauntings were a "ghostly representation of some long past tragedy." Lodge and others believed that violent emotions might somehow imprint themselves on their environment for later transmission to people sensitive enough to tune them in.

Perhaps it is not surprising, therefore, that stories of highly charged emotions seem to permeate the lore of hauntings. As examples on the following ten pages show, ghosts purportedly appear as fearsome harbingers of catastrophe or as specters of those whose passions in life left them unquiet in death—people with evil lusts or deep remorse or a thirst for justice or a need to play out endlessly the tragedy of thwarted love.

A Queen's Handmaiden

Looming atop a basalt crag that rises 250 feet above the Forth River, Stirling Castle was long held to be the mightiest fortress in Scotland. Because of its strategic central location, the poet Alexander Smith called it the "huge brooch" that "clasps Highlands and Lowlands together." The stone edifice that still stands today was built in the fifteenth century, replacing a timbered fort that towered above the surrounding plain some three hundred years before. Stirling was a favored residence for kings, and its windows afforded a panoramic view of battles crucial to the Scots' medieval wars for independence from England. The infant Mary Queen of Scots was crowned in its chapel in 1543, and she lived at Stirling from time to time as an adult.

Myriad ghosts are said to stalk the somber halls of Stirling, and many legends surround them. One concerns a Green Lady, who reportedly has often been seen by inmates of the castle, even in modern times. Some say that in life she was Queen Mary's maidservant and that she saved her mistress's life. The story goes that the girl, upon having a premonition that Mary was in danger, rushed to the queen's bedchamber and found flames consuming the massive draperies of the royal bed. The queen was sleeping, but the servant pulled her to safety. Afterward, Mary recounted a prophecy that a fire at Stirling would threaten her life.

Down through the centuries, appearances of the Green Lady were thought to herald fires and other disasters. Reportedly, she was seen most recently by a mess cook for troops then quartered in the castle. He claimed that while stirring soup he sensed that someone was watching him. Turning around, he saw the misty form of a woman who was dressed in green. No catastrophe ensued, although the mess cook did faint dead away.

A Feudal Lord's Tryst with Evil

Squat and massive, the sandstone ruins of Hermitage Castle crouch menacingly on the bleak Scottish moors near the English border. Legend says the castle's name derived from a religious recluse who started building a chapel on its site in the 1170s. The castle itself was completed in the thirteenth century by Nicholas de Soulis, head of a noble Norman family. It was Nicholas's son William who brought infamy—and some say hauntings—to Hermitage Castle.

According to old Border tales, William's passion was black magic. He studied with the master wizard Michael Scot and became in the process a ghoulish monster. In his dungeons, de Soulis reportedly murdered kidnapped children and used their blood in rituals that summoned a fanged demon, Robin Redcap. In return for the blood of young victims, Redcap guaranteed that de Soulis could be harmed neither by steel nor rope and was thus immune to the usual causes of violent death in that day. Deeming himself invulnerable, William terrorized the countryside with child murders and other outrages.

History indicates that de Soulis, after an unsuccessful plot to seize the Scottish crown from King Robert the Bruce, was consigned to prison and died there. But Border legend tells of a different fate. Supposedly, the local inhabitants took their grievances against de Soulis to King Robert. Irked by their repeated complaints, the king said, "Hang him, boil him, do anything you like to him, but for heaven's sake let me hear no more about him." Taking the monarch at his word, the people captured de Soulis, wrapped him in a sheet of lead, and boiled him in a cauldron.

William de Soulis's ghost supposedly was doomed to be summoned every seven years to the dungeons of Hermitage Castle. There, he meets Robin Redcap, who owns his soul. The evil pair reveal their presence in chilling screams and devilish laughter.

A Murderous Mother

Situated on the Thames some fifty miles west of London, Bisham Abbey is said to be the most haunted house in Berkshire. In its earliest form, the abbey was the thirteenth-century community house of the Knights Templars, a mystical-minded sect of medieval crusaders. Over the centuries, other owners expanded and embellished the mansion, which still stands today.

Resident there during Elizabethan times was the Hoby family, a titled assemblage of scholars and diplomats. Lady Elizabeth Hoby, well educated and brilliant, was a confidant of Queen Elizabeth I. According to legend, she was also a child murderer.

Lady Hoby supposedly had six children, among whom her youngest son, William, was an anomalous dullard, averse to any learning. He so angered his proud, ambitious mother with a messy lesson in his copybook that she beat him to death. Variations on the story say Lady Hoby locked the boy in a closet as punishment or tied him to a chair with directions to amend his work; she then went to visit the queen and returned days later to find him dead.

All versions of the brutal tale may be fables; no records exist of William's birth. Still, during renovations of the abbey in 1840, workmen found between the floor joists in the dining room some faded copybooks that bore signatures of the Hoby family. In one of them, the lessons were smudged and blotted on every page.

If Elizabeth Hoby did kill her son, she lived a long time with the guilt. By some accounts she died at eighty-one; by others she was in her nineties. And perhaps even death did not end her remorse. Among the ghosts reportedly seen at Bisham Abbey, Lady Hoby's shade is said to walk there with sorrowful mien. Before her floats a bowl of invisible water into which she dips her hands, trying like some spectral Lady Macbeth to wash away her guilt.

A White-Clad Baroness Seeks Revenge

Rising in ruined majesty beside the river Danube, the Bavarian fortress of Wolfsegg never fell to enemies in a history reaching back almost a thousand years. But while its walls withstood siege and strife without, they harbored violence within—mayhem said to echo still in the ghostly form of a woman who died there centuries ago.

Built in 1028, the fortress belonged successively to several quarrelsome Bavarian nobles, most of them involved in the region's incessant dynastic bickering. A Renaissance tale of triple murder surrounds one such aristocratic warrior clan, the Laabers of Wolfsegg. The story tells that in the fourteenth century, a Laaber baron married a lovely woman who became the victim of a nefarious plot. Wanting to take over the valuable estate, the baron's greedy relatives contrived to put the bride in a compromising situation with a man not her husband. The baron was then told that his wife was having an illicit rendezvous. He appeared at the castle to discover what looked to be a tryst, whereupon he killed his wife and her supposed lover. He, in turn, was murdered by the relatives, who claimed theirs was an act of justice.

Along with the feudal property, the relatives may have also inherited a curse; for some say the slain baroness, dressed in luminous white robes, still walks the halls and stairways of Wolfsegg. Residents of the castle have reported seeing glowing apparitions and hearing phantom footsteps and feeling inexplicable cold drafts.

Skeptics say the luminescences at Wolfsegg are mere will-o'-the-wisps, gaseous exudations from a bat-filled, dripstone cavern underlying the castle. But others believe that the White Lady returns to the site of her betrayal, seeking vindication of her name and justice for her traitorous kin.

A Tale of Love and Madness

Ornate gate pillars frame the ivied ruins of Baldoon Castle, which stands on a desolate stretch of the Scottish Lowlands some eighty miles south of Glasgow. In the mid-seventeenth century, Baldoon was the setting for a tragic tale that was later memorialized by Sir Walter Scott in his novel *The Bride of Lammermoor*.

The true story involved the family of Sir James Dalrymple, an eminent jurist and statesman. His eldest daughter was the beautiful Janet Dalrymple, who before she came of age, secretly pledged her troth to a poor young nobleman, Lord Rutherford. Janet's parents disapproved of the match. Particularly antagonistic was her mother, a haughty woman whose dictates even her husband dared not cross. Helpless before her mother's steely will, Janet broke faith with her true love and agreed to marry the man her parents chose for her—Rutherford's nephew, David Dunbar, the heir of Baldoon. With sad resignation, Janet married Dunbar on August 24, 1669.

There are several versions of what happened on Janet's wedding night, but the best known is this: There was a great bridal feast and ball at Baldoon, during which the bride and groom retired, as was the custom. Soon thereafter, wedding guests heard shrieks coming from the nuptial chamber. Breaking down its door, they found Dunbar lying across the threshold, blood streaming from stab wounds. His bride, her gown stained with his blood, was huddled in a corner, muttering to herself, obviously quite mad. The only coherent words she was heard to say were, "Tak up your bonny bridegroom." Dunbar survived, but Janet died within a month. It is said that her gore-dappled ghost still haunts Baldoon, perhaps in expiation, perhaps searching for her lost love.

CHAPTER 1

The Haunted World

A twenty-three-year-old actress from Germany named Elke Sommer was fast becoming a Hollywood film star when she and her husband, journalist Joe Hyams, bought a house in Beverly Hills, California, in 1964. Only days after they moved in, they began to experience unsettling—indeed, spooky—events. As Hyams later noted in a national-magazine article, neither he nor his wife shared the southern California proclivity for the supernatural: He was a tough-minded, fact-oriented journalist of fifteen years' experience, and she was a hardworking actress and practical woman "who once killed a rattlesnake in our backyard with a pair of garden shears." Nonetheless, what happened in their house over the next two years would finally convince the two levelheaded professionals of the existence of ghosts.

According to Hyams, the weird occurrences began on July 6, 1964, when Elke Sommer was visited by a German journalist, Edith Dahlfeld. As Sommer began to pour coffee, the journalist asked if her hostess was not going to introduce her to the man.

"What man?" asked Sommer. As far as she knew, her husband was not at home at the time.

"The one who was standing in the hall and just went into the dining room," Dahlfeld replied.

"It must be Joe," said Sommer, and went to look for him. There was no one else in the house, but the visiting journalist insisted that she had seen a husky man in dark slacks, a white shirt, and a black tie. He had a large "potato" nose—definitely not Joe Hyams. That evening the actress and her husband puzzled over the peculiar event and finally dismissed it, in Joe's words, as "one of those inexplicable things you shrug off and forget."

But two weeks later, Elke Sommer's mother—then staying with the Hyamses—reported that she had awakened in her downstairs bedroom to find a man at the foot of the bed, staring at her. Before she could scream, she said, the man disappeared. In the morning, Hyams convinced her that in her sleepy state she might have confused a prowler at the window for a man in the room. But when Hyams examined the ground beneath the window, it was smooth and unmarked, although rain the night before had made it soft.

At about this time, Hyams's account continues, the family began to hear a strange noise that was repeated almost every night: It was the sound of dining room chairs moving across the floor, as if diners had finished a meal and were pushing back from the table. And later that year, while Sommer was on location in Yugoslavia, Hyams continued to hear the nightly noises from the dining room and also found windows open that he had bolted the night before.

He decided to bug his own house. He purchased three miniature transmitters from an electronic detection specialty firm and set up three FM radios attached to tape recorders to receive and record the transmitters' signals. He hid one of the transmitters with its sensitive microphone at the entrance to the driveway to note the arrival of any intruder, secreted another near the front door to the house, and placed the third one in the dining room. Finally, he carefully positioned the chairs in the dining room and marked the locations of their feet on the floor with chalk.

That night, upstairs in the bedroom, he heard the by-now-familiar noises of chairs scraping on the dining room floor. Taking his .38 revolver from the night table, he quietly made his way down the stairs and along the hall to the open dining room door. Pointing the gun into the room with one hand, he flipped on the lights with the other. The dining room was still and silent. No one was present. The feet of every chair stood undisturbed within their chalked outlines. Hyams returned to his bedroom.

Later, listening to the tapes, he found no unexpected sounds from the transmitter by the house door or by the driveway. The tape of the sounds picked up by the dining

room transmitter told a different story, however. Hyams relates that it contained the noises of the moving furniture, which suddenly stopped with the snap of the light switch, and his own nervous cough as he peered into the room—and then, once he left, the sound of the chairs resuming their movement.

For more than a year thereafter, houseguests—some of them so terrified they departed immediately—reported glimpsing the heavyset man with the white shirt and black tie. Hyams and an architect equipped with blueprints carefully inspected the house, and a team of termite inspectors crawled under, over, and through every part of the structure to see whether there was some cranny or other space where an unwanted lodger, a residential stowaway, could live in secret or an unknown entrance that an interloper could use. There was neither. Furthermore, geologists and building contractors assured him that the house and the ground it was built on were not moving.

Hyams wondered if the whole experience was merely a matter of "overheated nerves reinforced by a few coincidences." But although he and his wife were reluctant to believe in a ghost, they did completely change the décor of the dining room when they were told that ghosts prefer familiar surroundings. The sounds continued. And the couple's dogs began behaving strangely, barking as they stared into the empty dining room, for example.

Hyams asked the Los Angeles branch of the American Society for Psychical Research for help. During the months that followed, he said, a series of "serious, and I believe, with few exceptions honest" mediums was ushered through the house by ASPR investigators, along with some interested scientists from UCLA. There were some striking similarities in the determinations of several of these sensitives, who were told no details of the Hyamses' experiences, not even who the owners of the house were.

One found the ghost to be a heavyset man, "a European, who spent his past life giving of himself." Two others came up with evidently the same large man of about fifty-eight years of age who had died of heart disease, one medium adding that he was a doctor who had died before completing a task with the "man of the house"—that is, Hyams. In fact, a few years earlier Hyams had been working on a book with a doctor of that age, who had died of a heart attack. But some findings varied markedly. Another sensitive discerned a large untidy man, what she termed a "monster," full of hate and "quite drunk." Yet another reported perceiving a young blond girl who had died of a lung problem and whose home had subsequently burned down. Sommer did have a young friend who had died some time before and whose house had later burned down.

By now, Sommer was terrified. Hyams found out that two previous owners of the house had sold it after brief tenancies—in both cases because the place was feared to be haunted. Eventually Hyams arranged for one of the mediums sent by the ASPR, Mrs. Lotte von Strahl, to come to "lay" the ghost—that is, to rid the house of it.

The exorcism was brief and businesslike. Seating herself at the head of the dining room table, von Strahl stated that the "horrible, brutal monster" was standing next to her. She asked Elke Sommer to join her in a short silent prayer, then addressed the ghost directly: "In the name of Jesus Christ I command you to leave this house at once. Leave these good people here alone and stop disturbing their house." After a few more words followed by a moment of silence, the medium declared in triumph: "He's leaving."

That night, Hyams and his wife locked the doors and windows and went to bed. Joe was just dozing off when Elke heard something. "Listen," she said. It was the sound of chairs moving in the dining room.

In his published account of those two years of harrow-

Joe Hyams and Elke Sommer stroll up the driveway of their California home, led by their dog Hasi—whose barking into an empty room was seen as a sign that the house was haunted. A detective employed to watch the place said locked doors and windows mysteriously opened and lights inexplicably turned on and off when no one was home.

ing nights and apparitions and sounds, Hyams wrote: "Even I am reluctantly convinced that we have at least one ghost in the house, but we don't intend to move out." Sommer felt the ghost was probably her father, and therefore was harmless. And Hyams went on to declare, "I would not let a living man frighten me out of my house, and I certainly don't intend to let a dead one do it."

About a year later, he had to back down from that defiant stance. According to Hyams, he and his wife were awakened early on the morning of March 13, 1967, by a loud banging at their bedroom door. Hyams later reported that he heard what he thought was laughter sounding from downstairs as he picked up his pistol and opened the door. He found no one there but saw that smoke was billowing up the stairs from the ground floor. Hurriedly escaping out a bedroom window and down a roof that sloped almost to ground level, the couple discovered their dining room was engulfed by a furiously hot blaze that arson investigators later attributed to "mysterious origins." Neither the fire nor the loud knocking that saved the couple's lives could be explained. But enough was enough. Joe Hyams reconsidered his pledge to stay and put the house up for sale.

From Hyams's description, it appears that he and Elke Sommer experienced a classic haunting—not in a tradition-

al setting, an ancient castle, say, on the edge of a lonely British moor, but in a modern dwelling situated in a busy urban community. In the land of freeways and television studios and aerospace assembly lines, under the smog-refracted glare of the southern California sun, the couple gained an unwelcome personal familiarity with some of the dark elements that have been the stuff of ghost stories for centuries and that psychical investigators have found are characteristic of houses or other sites that come to be labeled haunted.

Sometimes called localized psi effects (psi being a catchall adjective applied to events that are apparently psychic or parapsychological in nature), these classic elements may include an apparition of a person or an animal that reportedly keeps reappearing, usually in the same place, and that is visible to one or more people, although not to everyone. Descriptions of such phantoms range from wispy wraiths glimpsed only from the corner of the eye to convincingly solid-looking figures such as the heavyset man reported in Elke Sommer's house.

The recurring quality of the apparition—it is reported to have been seen again and again over a period of time—is important in distinguishing a haunting from another kind of psi event involving what is called a crisis apparition. A crisis apparition generally is said to appear only once, and the image is that of a person known to the percipient, usually a close friend or relative. The percipient often learns later that the phantom appeared just as the individual it represented was undergoing a crisis—a mother sees a vision of her soldier-son at the moment of his wounding, for instance, or at the time of his death. Some researchers who believe in ESP suggest a crisis apparition results from a powerful telepathic message transmitted to the percipient by the person whose image appears.

A haunting apparition, on the other hand, is associated with a particular place, rather than a particular percipient. It may be perceived by several different people, and perhaps none of them will recognize it as any specific per-

Theories of Apparitions

Haunting apparitions—ghosts—traditionally have been considered spirits of the dead, although skeptics have long had doubts. In Shakespeare's time, one of his characters could reasonably dismiss a ghost as "but our fantasy." And Charles Dickens reflected a Victorian view when his Ebenezer Scrooge attributed a phantom to an upset stomach, accusing the ghost of being "an undigested bit of beef."

For the past century or so, however, students of the paranormal have been diligently seeking other explanations. None of their theories has satisfied the skeptics, however, who insist that most alleged haunting phenomena are unsubstantiated anyway. But although the proposed explanations have not been proved, some have a certain ring of reasonableness that keeps them alive. The basic elements of a few of those theories, along with the older, Spiritualist belief, are given here.

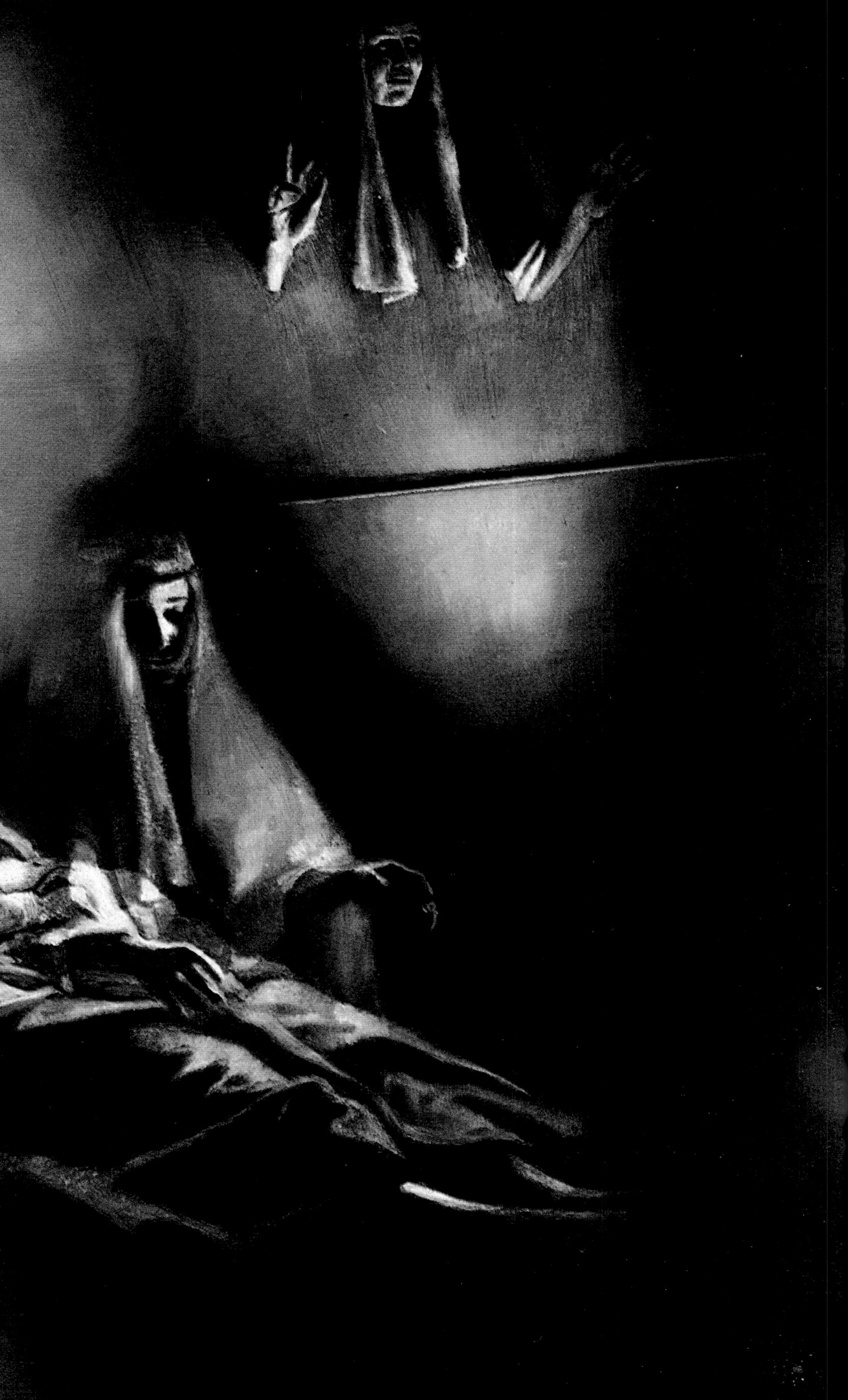

Spiritualists believe that the soul leaves the body at death, as shown here. Under certain circumstances, this spirit may tarry on earth instead of proceeding to the Other Side and thus may be observed as a ghost. Italian psychical researcher Ernesto Bozzano put a new twist on this explanation with his "spiritistic" theory. Apparitions, Bozzano proposed, are not the souls of the dead, but rather telepathic messages from their lingering bodiless minds, which he said have many of the characteristics usually attributed to spirits.

As symbolized at left by an eye that both projects and observes a ghost's image, the mind of a percipient may create the very apparition that it perceives, according to American parapsychologist William G. Roll. Roll accepts that stored psychic traces from the past can evoke apparitions. But he contends that in many cases the percipient's mental state plays an active role, unconsciously creating haunting phenomena to satisfy emotional needs.

In the symbolic illustration at upper left, an apparition emerges from a wall where it has been stored as a trace of psychic energy. According to this theory, first posited by the researcher Eleanor Sidgwick, objects absorb psychic impressions and then broadcast them back to people who enter the vicinity. Clarity of the resulting apparition or other phenomena depends on the emotional force of the original psychic imprint and the psychic sensitivity of the percipient.

In Oxford University professor Henry Habberley Price's "psychic ether" theory, an image born of mental activity lives on in another plane or in multiple planes (right), even after its creator has died. Price said that the ether was "something intermediate between mind and matter" that exists in a dimension or dimensions unknown to us. It is this ether, not our physical environment, he suggested, that records psychic impressions and plays them back to psychically sensitive people.

son. In the Hyams-Sommer case, the recurrent localized apparition—or ghost, to use a more common if less precise term—seemed to be associated with the dining room. None of the people who said they saw the heavyset man recognized him. Sometimes, however, a haunting phantom is reported to resemble a known deceased individual.

According to Hyams's account, the case was also characterized by another prime element of classic hauntings: a noise that mimics the sound of a human activity. In this instance, the imitative noise, as researchers term it, was the sound of chairs scraping on the floor. Furniture being moved around is a commonly reported audible feature of hauntings. (Footsteps that cross the floor or go up or down stairs is another; so is the crash of breaking dishes.)

The reaction of the couple's dogs, barking into the dining room, fits the classic mold too. In the popular mind, a dog snarling or barking at an empty chair or into an unoccupied room or corner has long signified the presence of ghosts, and modern investigators have found that displays of agitation or fear in animals are statistically part of the pattern of phenomena known as hauntings. Hyams also found windows open that he believed had been locked, another characteristic occurrence; in some cases, witnesses claim to observe doors or windows being opened, as if by unseen hands that turn the knobs or move the latch handles. And most haunting occurrences take place at night, as did the majority—but not all—of the events in the Beverly Hills house.

Whatever was disturbing the domestic tranquillity of Joe Hyams and Elke Sommer did omit some of the classic phenomena associated with hauntings. No one reported seeing any balls of light or other strange luminosities. There was no unexplained tugging at the bedclothes. Peculiarly cold areas in a house are also frequently reported, as is a sulfurous odor or other distinct smell. The Hyamses experienced neither.

They did suffer a dangerous fire, however. If there truly was a paranormal pattern at work in the house and if the unexplained blaze in the dining room was yet another ele-

ment in it, then at least part of what the couple experienced would properly be considered a poltergeist phenomenon, rather than a traditional haunting. Poltergeist manifestations involve more noise and movement of physical objects—sometimes violent movement—than do other hauntings. Most hauntings are disturbing for those experiencing them but present no actual danger. If the fire was of paranormal origin, the Hyamses were being subjected to a rare and extremely frightening kind of haunting—one that threatens or deals real physical harm to the percipients.

Finally, their response to the experience also is in keeping with the classic haunting pattern: They sought help in trying to "lay the ghost," to rid the house of the disturbances that were plaguing their lives. People have been practicing exorcism and other techniques for banishing what they take to be troublesome spirits for as long as hauntings have been known.

Apparently, they have been known for a very long time, probably from the earliest era in which human beings were capable of conceiving of ghosts. Certainly haunting was a well-established phenomenon by the fourth century BC, when the Greek philosopher Plato wrote of "the soul which survives the body." Sometimes, he said, this soul is wrapped in an "earthy covering, which makes it heavy and visible, and drags it down to the visible region. . . . And thus these wandering souls haunt, as we call it, the tombs and monuments of the dead, where such phantoms are sometimes seen."

One of the earliest recorded hauntings was believed caused by the ghost of a traitorous fifth-century-BC Spartan commander named Pausanias, who took sanctuary in a temple of Athena and was starved to death there. The ghost terrified worshipers at the temple with unearthly noises until it was exorcised by a necromancer.

The nature of hauntings has not changed much over the centuries. "There are plenty of houses haunted by these spirits and goblins, which ceaselessly disturb the sleep of those who dwell in them," a Frenchman named Pierre Le Loyer wrote almost 400 years ago. "They will stir and overturn the utensils, vessels, tables, boards, dishes, bowls, . . . throw stones, enter chambers, . . . pull the curtains and coverlets, and perpetuate a thousand tricks." But the spirits do no real harm, he wrote, "for the household vessels all of which they seem to have smashed and broken, are found the next morning to be intact."

Interestingly, the percentage of people who experience alleged haunting phenomena has also remained fairly constant, at least if surveys bracketing the last hundred years or so are a valid indication. Britain's Society for Psychical Research polled a large sampling of people soon after its founding in 1882 and found that some 10 percent of them said they had had an inexplicable experience—seeing or hearing or being touched by what seemed to be a living being or inanimate object when no such being or object was present in reality. Similar surveys taken in the 1970s in the United States, Britain, and Iceland produced positive responses from 9 to 17 percent of those questioned. And most of those who reported seeing, hearing, or otherwise experiencing an apparition said they did so in their own homes, rather than in some eerie, cobwebbed location of the kind popularly thought likely to be haunted.

"The tea-party question, 'Do you believe in ghosts?' is one of the most ambiguous which can be asked," wrote Henry Habberley Price, emeritus professor of logic at Oxford University and ardent psychical researcher who twice served as president of the SPR. "But if we take it to mean 'Do you believe that people sometimes experience apparitions?', the answer is that they certainly do. No one who examines the evidence can come to any other conclusion. Instead of disputing the facts, we must try to explain them."

The first systematic attempt to explain apparitions and other features of hauntings began with the founding of the Society for Psychical Research. The early researchers—mostly academics from various fields—started by collecting hundreds of personal accounts and attempting to weed out those incidents that could be attributed to natural causes, fraud, or unreliable sources. Whenever possible, SPR inves-

tigators made efforts to observe the phenomena firsthand.

One who achieved an especially intimate experience of a haunting was an SPR member named G. A. Smith, who in 1888 moved with his wife into a small house in the seaside resort of Brighton on England's south coast. Apparently the society instigated, perhaps even subsidized, the Smith family's move in order to make closer inspection of haunting phenomena that reportedly had plagued residents of the house for some years.

The first occupant whose troubles had come to the SPR's attention was pseudonymously identified in reports as a Miss L. Morris. (Researchers routinely identify those who allegedly experience haunting phenomena by pseudonyms, to protect them from publicity.) Miss Morris had moved into the house in 1882 and evidently was a plucky young woman. Upon hearing unusual noises in her new home, she would arm herself with a poker and march from room to room to challenge the unseen intruder. She heard persistent heavy footsteps and banging, but the most alarming imitative noise during her tenancy was the violent, uncontrolled ringing of the doorbell. It was an old-fashioned, mechanical apparatus with an outside handle connected by a pull-wire to a bell within the house; when a caller moved the handle, the connecting wire shook the bell and made it ring. In her first two years in the house, Miss Morris experienced a number of what she called runaway rings, in which she answered the bell to find no one there; she put it down to pranksters who rang and then ran away.

But beginning in June 1884, "for three weeks, at intervals of a quarter of an hour or a half an hour, it rang incessantly, and such peals, it electrified us." Members of the household stood watch at the open door to see that no one was there, but the bell kept ringing anyway. Finally Miss Morris ordered the bell taken out. Later, after it was removed, she must have felt a chill along her spine when she and her servants saw the disconnected bell wire continuing to vibrate "as if the bell were attached to it." Nonetheless, the indomitable Miss Morris stayed two more years before

Capturing Ghosts on Film

Since the invention of the camera, people have been trying to take photographs of ghosts. What, after all, could be greater proof of a phantom's existence than its image on film? The efforts have led mainly to failure and fakery, however.

The fakery was introduced in the early days of photography, which coincided with the heyday of Spiritualism. In 1861, Boston photographer William Mumler started shooting portraits that included dim images alleged to be his customers' deceased loved ones. Business boomed until it was noted that the ghost faces resembled some living Bostonians and could have been double exposures or overprinted images. Mumler was arrested, but fraudulent "spirit photography" of one kind or another continued to flourish.

Still, sometimes an alleged ghost photo turns up with at least a persuasive provenance, if not an ironclad one. The pictures presented here all lay claim to being legitimate. In each case, the photographer professed to be surprised by the result.

Miss Sybell Corbet said that she was shocked when the picture below revealed a vague figure sitting in the chair in the foreground, since the room—the library of Wellington Henry, Viscount Combermere— had been unoccupied when she made the exposure in 1891. She was even more astonished by the figure's resemblance to the recently deceased Lord Combermere, who was being buried on the day the photograph was taken.

But her surprise is hard to credit, since the exposure lasted an hour and she left her camera unattended during that time. The result is consistent with someone entering and sitting in the chair for half a minute. The butler insisted, however, that no one entered the room while the picture was being made.

An expert who examined the photo above said the image of Mabel Chinnery's dead mother in the rear seat could not be a reflection or overprint. "I stake my reputation on the fact that the picture is genuine," he declared.

Mrs. Mabel Chinnery expressed similar surprise in 1959 when she saw the picture above. After photographing her mother's grave, she took a picture of her husband. He was alone in his car at the time, but the developed snapshot showed Mrs. Chinnery's mother in the backseat. A photographic expert who examined the photo for a British paper declared it genuine.

In 1966, retired Canadian clergyman Ralph Hardy photographed an elegant spiral staircase *(right)* at the National Maritime Museum in Greenwich, England. When the picture was developed, he claimed to be amazed to see the image of a hooded figure climbing the stairs. Experts allegedly concluded no one had tampered with the negative.

The figure thought to be the ghost of Lord Combermere, who had died after being run over by a horse-drawn cab, is in the chair at left in this photo of the Combermere Abbey library. Skeptics think a servant sat briefly in the chair during the long exposure.

At far right, a supposed specter climbs the stairs with both hands on the banister. The underside of the spiral stairs is at left.

moving out and added to her experiences the reported sighting of a female apparition with a pale, sad face.

After standing vacant for a year, the house was taken by a widow, Mrs. Gilby (again a pseudonym), and her two children. The reconnected doorbell gave Mrs. Gilby the same kind of trouble. But worse, within two weeks of moving in, she heard sobs and moans one night, accompanied by deep thumps. Checking their bedrooms, she found her children and her maid sound asleep. She roused the maid, and for the rest of the night the two women heard sobs and moans and a voice—"a sweet one"—repeating the phrase, "Oh, do forgive me!" Within six months, a distraught Mrs. Gilby moved out, but not before reporting that she, too, had seen a "pale woman's face."

Two of the SPR's foremost researchers of that era, Edmund Gurney and Frank Podmore, investigated the case. Both were respected as men of unquestioned probity. Gurney was a classical scholar and fellow of Trinity College, Cambridge; Podmore was a career civil servant. Between them, they eventually interviewed four independent sets of witnesses who testified to observing the same kind of phenomena in the house. But in this case the SPR did not have to rely on others; it was able to place on the scene its own man, G. A. Smith, who had been Gurney's secretary.

It is typical in the annals of hauntings that when investigators arrive in person to see what is going on, the phantasms and related manifestations suddenly take a vacation, perhaps because the researchers disturb the psychic atmosphere, or perhaps because the reports were not that accurate in the first place. But that was far from true in this case. Smith not only filled his punctilious diary with details of many strange events during the thirteen months he lived in the house, he and his wife also played host to no fewer than 137 overnight guests, most of them SPR members eager to have a firsthand experience of a haunting. They were not disappointed. The doorbell continued its errant ringing, and

Willington Mill House, the small gabled structure in the center, appears to be nestling against the big flour mill, but the residence in fact was completely detached— a key consideration to investigators of reported hauntings there.

there was a frequent tapping noise on the floor that sounded like a hammer "using enough force to drive tacks in"; also reported was the sound of someone dragging a brick across the linoleum.

On December 15, 1888, the Smiths witnessed an event that even the sophisticated SPR man found "most remarkable and inexplicable." At about 11:35 p.m. his wife was saying her prayers in the sitting room while Smith climbed into bed in the adjoining bedroom. Suddenly a guitar that hung on the sitting room wall emitted three distinct musical notes, which Smith characterized as "pung, pang, ping." As his wife called out to him, "Did you hear that?" the guitar repeated the musical phrase twice. Mrs. Smith averred that during the second and third performances she was staring directly at the instrument but saw nothing there that could cause it to play—no person, no mouse, nothing. Smith pointed out that the sound could not have been the guitar's tuning pegs slipping, since that would have changed the frequencies and thus the notes as the strings slackened.

Having completed their study of the house, the Smiths moved out in September of 1889. When interviewed the next year, subsequent tenants reported no further psychic activity. The Smiths seem not to have suffered any notable trauma during their firsthand haunting investigation. In fact, Smith's diary indicates he enjoyed a certain restrained excitement during his experiences. In another case that the SPR reported not long after that, however, a decidedly skeptical man of science who became directly involved in a haunting investigation finished his participation in a state of utter panic.

The SPR published an account of that case in 1891, when the diary of a chief participant became available, but the events actually transpired some decades earlier. The incidents happened in the residence adjacent to the Willington Mill, near Tyneside in the north of England, starting in the fall of 1834. The house was inhabited by a Quaker family named Procter. (Mr. Procter's was the diary that provided details of the case.) All the family members said they heard footsteps, whistles, the sound of a clock being wound, and angry stomping, along with voices. Beds were alleged to rise up and tremble in the night. A neighbor reported seeing a transparent, white apparition of a woman in a window, and thereafter the same phantasm was said to appear to the family on different occasions. Other accounts told of a white face that sometimes watched the inhabitants over a stair rail. This went on for some six years until a local doctor, Edward Drury, got wind of it and asked Procter's permission to spend the night in the house. He arrived with his friend T. Hudson on July 3, 1840, at a time when the family was away; armed with a brace of pistols, he "sat down on the third floor landing, fully expecting to account for any noises [he] might hear in a philosophical manner."

Dr. Drury said later that he had to wait only about fifty minutes before he heard the patter of feet, then the sound of someone knocking on the floor and a hollow cough. Things quieted down and Drury's companion, Hudson, fell asleep on the floor. At about ten minutes to one in the morning, Drury's eyes "became rivetted upon a closet door, which [he] distinctly saw open, and saw also the figure of a female attired in greyish garments, with the head inclining downwards." The wraith advanced toward him. Screaming, Drury lunged at the figure. But instead of coming to grips with the phantom, he fell on top of his sleeping friend and recollected "nothing distinctly for nearly three hours afterwards." He wrote later, "I have since learned that I was carried downstairs in an agony of fear and terror." Procter noted the next day that Dr. Drury "has got a shock he will not soon cast off."

The haunting phenomena finally drove the Procters from the house in 1847. Later occupants reported some strange noises, but by 1890 the hauntings seemed to have ceased. The house was later demolished.

As the results of many such investigations were published and discussed over the years, attempts to explain apparitions produced a multitude of theories and even more questions. Eleanor Sidgwick, a mathematician who was principal of Newnham College, Cambridge, and who happened to be the sister of British prime minister A. J. Balfour, coordinated the SPR's first major study of the subject. She articulated one of the primary questions early on: Does an apparition exist independently of people, that is, is it there even if no one is around to perceive it? Or is it some form of communication from a sending source that requires the presence of a percipient?

Spiritualists have offered the answer that an apparition is indeed an independent entity—the disembodied spirit of a deceased individual. This, of course, is the popular explanation for ghosts. Some who embrace this theory say the spirit is earthbound because it wants something, others that it is here simply from habit or because it is insane. Some theorize that it creates a visible presence from energy that it somehow draws from living beings and even from plants if no human or other animal life is accessible.

Many of the leading parapsychologists who have pondered the question of hauntings have rejected as unscientific the idea of a spirit that survives bodily death. But some of the alternative explanations they have suggested seem equally difficult to prove scientifically, even if possessed of a degree of logical consistency.

In 1919, one of Italy's leading experts on psychic phenomena, Ernesto Bozzano, proposed that a person's mind—the individual's whole complex of thought and mental experience—might somehow have an existence beyond corporeal life and could become trapped in an earthly setting after the subject's death. In such a case, the disembodied mind would function as a telepathic agent, sending mental messages that would make noise or move objects or cause living people to see its form.

Frederic W. H. Myers, like Gurney a Trinity College classical scholar and one of the founders of the SPR, noted that the reported behavior of phantoms often resembles the repetitive, seemingly pointless, movements and utterances of figures in dreams, rather than the coherent and deliberate actions of a person who is awake. He suggested the possibility that apparitions were not the dead themselves, but the dreams of the deceased. Just as the effects of a physical action can persist after the action itself has ended, Myers postulated, so might the effects of a mental action such as dreaming. The persisting dream somehow causes the percipient to hallucinate the dream's image.

Hallucination, of course, has a role in many theories about hauntings. But even parapsychologists who believe that all apparitions are hallucinations, in that they are without solid physical form, have questions and conflicting notions about both the causes and the mechanism of the hallucinatory process.

If an apparition is a hallucination, how is it that several percipients sometimes see the same phantom at the same time—or at different times? Some researchers have theorized that one person first experiences the subjective hallucination that constitutes a haunting and then passes it on telepathically to others. One such notion suggests the telepathic message sent out by the original hallucinator may linger in the atmosphere to cause others to perceive the apparition later.

But what of those cases of "veridical hallucinations," in which the percipients learn something from the apparition about the dead person it represents—details of appearance, perhaps, or biographical facts—that later research verifies? How can these true details, previously unknown to percipients, be part of a subjective hallucination?

To account for such cases, students of the subject have proposed various ways in which psychic energy could persist beyond the lifetime of its originator. Eleanor Sidgwick suggested that the structure of a house itself could absorb psychic impressions from people who have lived in it. These stored messages would then trigger a psychic reaction in the minds of people who later entered the house, especially psychically sensitive people. (This is akin to the idea of psychometry, in which a medium claims the ability to gain information by "reading" psychic vibrations from an object such as a tie clip or a watch.)

A very old structure presumably might carry an especially powerful charge of psychic impressions, because of

Phantoms of the Footlights

By all accounts, ghosts abound in London's West End theaters. Theatrical promoters, of course, probably encourage reports of hauntings for a boost at the box office. But so many different people—audience, staff, and actors—have claimed to witness haunting phenomena there that it is difficult to dismiss all the stories as hoaxes.

Dozens of people, for instance, have reported seeing the unidentified "man in gray" who is said to haunt the upper circle of the Theatre Royal, Drury Lane. The specter of the late Sir Charles Wyndham, first owner of the New Theatre (later renamed the Albery), has been reported backstage there, and an apparition of an anguished woman wringing her hands like Lady Macbeth is said to appear at the Old Vic.

Actress Margaret Rutherford of Miss Marple fame was among many who have reported encounters in the Haymarket Theatre with the phantom of John Buckstone, manager of that house until his death in 1879.

During a popular musical revue at the Haymarket in 1963, a stage manager was horrified to see a man he took to be an errant stagehand standing directly behind a performer. He was about to order the curtain dropped to get the culprit offstage when the figure suddenly disappeared. The stage manager then realized the man had been wearing a long frock coat and resembled descriptions of Buckstone.

Among the most famous supposed theater ghosts is that of William Terriss, leading man in production after production at the Adelphi Theatre during the late nineteenth century. He was adored by crowds and critics alike but inspired a fanatical envy in a bit player, Richard Prince, who on December 16, 1897, stabbed Terriss in the chest as the star approached the stage door. Dying in the arms of his leading lady, Terriss was heard to whisper, "I shall come back."

Many contend that Terriss kept his word. Over the decades, strange lights and rapping noises have allegedly emanated from his old dressing rooms. And his apparition has been reported not only in the theater but in the nearby Charing Cross underground station, where he often waited for a late train home. Descriptions consistently have included details of Terriss's frock coat, top hat, and walking stick. But witnesses say that when they try to speak to the specter, it vanishes immediately.

Actor William Terriss (below) has been called the first matinée idol. Since his murder in 1897, his ghost has been reported in the Adelphi Theatre, shown at left as it looked during the 1800s.

the long time that they have been accumulating. If true, then that might account for the number of ancient castles and mansions alleged to be haunted. An excellent example is Wildenstein Castle, a fifteenth-century building that stands near Heilbronn in West Germany. There, a long list of people over many generations, including visitors, staff, and owners, have claimed they experienced an astonishing spectrum of eerie events.

Typical was a reported occurrence in 1945, just after World War II ended, when American soldiers were billeted at the castle. An officer was taking a bath one day when the bathroom door suddenly opened and a young woman in white came in. The officer told her to leave, but she stood there, staring at him. Unnerved, he got out of the tub and tried to push her out the door—but his hand passed through her. The apparition then vanished, and the officer ran naked and terrified into the kitchen to report his experience.

Legend tells of haunting activity at the castle for centuries past. But the earliest written accounts date from the 1850s, according to Hans Bender, a German parapsychologist who studied Wildenstein in great depth. In that era, a member of the staff, having seen an apparition of a man pulling a chain past his door, refused thereafter to sleep in the building, as did a teacher who was frightened one night by an unexplained "great noise." The wife of a policeman noted a shadowy woman while hearing the rustle of silk dragging across the floor. In the 1920s, a visiting curate, who was taking part in a musical evening there, saw flames licking a wall, but the fire disappeared as he watched. Phantom music was frequently heard, right up to the 1950s when the castle was in the hands of Maximilian, Baron Hofer von Lobenstein—a nobleman who worked as medical superintendent of a nearby hospital—and his wife, Anneliese. The baroness said that one day when her husband was away,

she saw a little boy in a sailor suit across the kitchen table from her, gazing at her in a friendly fashion. She wrote the baron about it, and he responded that she had most likely seen Little Adolph, a boy who had died of diphtheria in 1890, at the age of six. Maximilian said she could find a picture of the boy in a storeroom. She found the picture and noted a considerable resemblance to the phantom child in the kitchen—an indication, if not conclusive evidence, that the apparition was veridical, or verifiable. Visitors to the castle often said they heard a child crying in the night.

The baron reported that on one occasion he was putting his dogs out at about 11:00 p.m., when he was astonished to see a tiny man with a beard standing about ten feet away. Thinking it was a reflection, the baron went inside and turned off the lights. But when he went outside again, he said, the figure, which he took to be a goblin, was still there and cavorted around him for a few minutes before disappearing. He did not believe in goblins, his wife later reported to Bender, and was "quite angry" about seeing one. Subsequently, the baroness herself reported seeing the goblin for an instant—in broad daylight.

Because the various alleged paranormal events

at Wildenstein Castle were not limited to a single percipient, or even to generations of a single family, but were experienced by many different observers over a long period, said Bender, "we ought to suppose . . . that some action or event provoking strong emotions among the persons concerned, creates an atmosphere attached to the spot, but independent from people, and that this atmosphere causes paranormal events or favors their taking place." This is, of course, a viewpoint not all that different from Eleanor Sidgwick's theory of houses soaking up psychic impressions.

Professor H. H. Price suggested the possibility that it is not the actual physical structure of a building that preserves the messages, but what he called a psychic ether, a coexisting dimension that is invisible but lies alongside or among the dimensions with which we are familiar. This ever-present dimension, he speculated, could be very sensitive to psychic impressions and register them somewhat in the manner of movie film. Most of the impressions would be trivial, but a deeply emotional experience would register strongly, much as a high-contrast scene registers sharply on film, and would be more easily discerned later by an exceptionally sensitive person. The other-dimensional scene may replay itself over and over with the repetitiveness often associated with hauntings.

Andrew MacKenzie, a prolific paranormal researcher and writer in England, does not think that "any intelligent agency," deceased or otherwise, operates in most haunting cases. But he does agree that "a subtle interaction between a person, or family, and a house or area" is the cause of many hauntings. "Some places are imbued with feeling or atmosphere—call it what you will—which may be experienced by a sensitive person, although not by others, and this interaction of person and place can result in hallucinations in which apparitions are seen or footsteps or strange sounds heard."

The importance of a percipient's sensitivity to psychic signals is evident in a series of incidents that took place in Ardachie Lodge, some miles from Glasgow, in the 1950s. P. J. M. McEwan, a member of the SPR who was trained in psychology at Edinburgh University, bought the house in 1952. It had previously been inhabited by a "Mrs. B.," a paralyzed invalid who also suffered from mental illness. She had eventually been hospitalized and had died about three years before McEwan and his wife arrived. The McEwans had no unusual experiences in Ardachie Lodge until a couple named Mathews came to work there as domestics on August 17, 1953.

The new servants, Londoners who had never been in that area before, retired early on their first night but soon returned downstairs to tell the McEwans they had both distinctly heard footsteps outside their room, even though no one was there. The McEwans shrugged off the incident, and the Mathewses returned to bed—only to come rushing back to their employers about twenty minutes later. This time, they claimed, they had heard rapping on the wall and were convinced that something supernatural was afoot. Mr. McEwan and Mr. Mathews then sat in the servants' room in the dark for a time, but they heard nothing. The Mathewses

Looming over the German countryside, Wildenstein Castle was the scene of storied hauntings for many centuries. But no paranormal phenomena have been reported there since it became a youth hostel in the 1970s.

asked for another room nonetheless, and it was provided.

Immediately on entering the new room, Mrs. Mathews grew agitated and said, "There's a woman in this room." Her body stiffened, and she stared into a corner of the brightly lit room as if in a trance. After a few moments, she gathered herself together, as if waking from a dream, and said she had seen an old woman with a cap and a shawl beckoning to her.

The McEwans arranged yet another room for the Mathewses, but within minutes after retiring the servants roused them again. This time the frightened pair had heard tapping on the bed's headboard, above Mrs. Mathews's head. When the foursome then entered the new room together, Mrs. Mathews became rigid again. She said she was again seeing the old woman, who now was crawling toward her on hands and knees.

The Mathewses did not remain long at the lodge, but the McEwans took the opportunity to study the alleged haunting of the servant couple while they could. Two other SPR members joined them. At night the group maintained a vigil in the Mathewses' bedroom, monitoring Mrs. Mathews's restlessness and her reports of rapping and noting that she tended to sleep with her hand knotted tightly in a fist, her arm rigid. McEwan eventually decided that Mrs. Mathews was probably "psychologically unbalanced."

But by then the McEwans also knew that Mrs. Mathews's description of the apparition she saw matched almost exactly the appearance of the invalid who had previously owned Ardachie Lodge. They had learned that toward the end the paralytic old woman had taken to crawling on all fours to get around the house—just as Mrs. Mathews had described. And after Mrs. Mathews reported that she felt especially uncomfortable in a particular part of the garden, the McEwans discovered that the previous owner had spent much time in that corner tending her beloved roses. These were things that the Mathewses, who were new to the area, simply could not have known about. The apparition seemed truly veridical.

In his report to the journal of the SPR, McEwan stated his belief that "paranormal activity had occurred and that it was made possible by the mental state" of Mrs. Mathews. After the London couple departed, no more haunting phenomena were reported in Ardachie Lodge. Although the apparition apparently possessed verifiable aspects that indicated it could not have been purely Mrs. Mathews's hallucination, it seemed to depend on her psychic sensitivity in order to be perceived.

Another British case carries the importance of a percipient's paranormal gifts a step further, suggesting that a psychically sensitive individual may summon presences so strong that they are then perceived by other people—and are perhaps more substantial than mere visual apparitions.

The case was investigated by the experienced Dutch parapsychologist George Zorab, who first discovered it, and by MacKenzie, who conducted interviews about the events and collaborated with Zorab on a published report. It involved a young woman identified as Thelma Graham, who grew up in a house on London's outskirts. A maid, called Mrs. Turner in the report, began working at the house in 1965, when Thelma, the youngest of three daughters, was ten years old. Soon after taking the job, Mrs. Turner reportedly felt a presence in the house, often sensing that it wanted to pass her on the stairs. Later, when Thelma was about twenty years old, Mrs. Turner once allegedly felt the presence physically pushing her; disturbed by the experience, she left the Grahams' employ.

Meanwhile, according to the report, Thelma had begun to see a female figure flitting around the upstairs and to hear loud clattering noises coming from the kitchen at night. And George Wells, her sister's husband, who happened to be visiting, was said to have awoke in the dark one night to see the figure of a woman reaching up toward the top of the wardrobe in his bedroom, as if dusting it; she was dressed in what seemed to be the uniform of a nineteenth-century servant. Thelma's mother, too, reportedly experienced strange events: She sometimes heard doors opening and closing and once, while talking on the telephone, watched in fright as a door opened about a foot without any apparent human assistance, then closed and opened again, repeating the action five times in all.

Some parapsychologists say that emotional tension in a household is a common element that can be found in most cases of hauntings and poltergeists. Thelma Graham had what both she and her parents described as a difficult adolescence. She went out more often than her parents liked, which led to frequent squabbles. Apparently, she also suffered from a mild case of anorexia—a disorder characterized by self-inflicted undernourishment and a complex of attendant emotional problems that is most common among appearance-conscious teenage girls. Psychical investigator George Zorab believes that the troubled Thelma provided an "energy centre" in the house, that she had—unbeknown to herself—the paranormal powers of a medium and in her emotionally disturbed state was bringing forth the haunting phenomena. Zorab says that the phenomena summoned in such a manner are not necessarily mere subjec-tive hallucinations, but may possess "mass and objectivity."

If such was the case here, is it possible that Thelma's energy somehow gave substance to lingering psychic traces of a maid who had worked in the house in an earlier era? Could Thelma have given the apparition such tangible substance that it not only was seen by her brother-in-law and caused a door to open and close in the presence of her mother, but actually pushed Mrs. Turner, who now held the long-dead-maid's job?

Andrew MacKenzie describes such hauntings as "manifestations of an aspect of reality of which at present we have only glimmerings of understanding." But a leading American parapsychologist, William G. Roll, believes that humanity's understanding has progressed beyond glimmerings to a somewhat more concrete stage. He outlines an all-inclusive explanation for hauntings in which a number of causes differing by degrees are ranged along a spectrum.

At one end of the spectrum, says Roll, are cases where haunting images or sounds can be clearly related to a par-

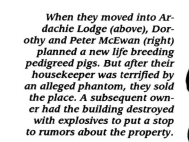

When they moved into Ardachie Lodge (above), Dorothy and Peter McEwan (right) planned a new life breeding pedigreed pigs. But after their housekeeper was terrified by an alleged phantom, they sold the place. A subsequent owner had the building destroyed with explosives to put a stop to rumors about the property.

ticular person or event—the sudden death of a former occupant of a house, say. "These kinds of occurrences seem to leave an imprint in the environment that a lot of people can respond to," he says. "The source of the localized effect is a strong, memory-like trace imprinted in the physical environment." Roll says that to comprehend this kind of imprinted memory, "we don't have to talk about psychic ether," but just accept that "the memories are *there.*"

"Events that would give us strong memories in our minds—death, accidents and so forth—are the same kind that are strong outside our bodies," he says. "All we need to say is that there is no sharp distinction between mind and matter, and that the processes that go on in the human brain may also go on in the human environment. To me the main interest of these phenomena is that they suggest body and mind and mind and matter are not as clearly distinguished as we have been led to believe, that mind is enfolded in matter, that there is meaning in matter, that the physical environment has mental qualities that come from the people who have lived in that environment."

At the other end of the spectrum, according to Roll, "is another type of haunting, where it's the percipient who may be the source." Typically, he says, this situation may develop when "a family is out of balance; the husband is away a lot, leaving the wife alone with the baby, or they've had a falling out and enjoy no intimate relationship." In that kind of case, he suggests, "an objective reality," a sort of quasi personality, is sometimes created to fill the space.

"It's like a dream that has become real," the researcher explains, "a strong need that somehow has created a situation that satisfies it. My impression is that memories will be drawn out in response to needs. And it is just as likely to happen in a new duplex as an old mansion." Other cases find their position along Roll's spectrum according to the relative strength of the two forces involved, the lingering psychic trace on the one hand and the needs of the percipient on the other.

A series of reported haunting occurrences that took place neither in an old mansion nor in a new duplex, but in the unlikely setting of a radio station, may serve as an example of Roll's combination of causes—psychic trace and percipients' needs—at work. In 1981, the manager of a Virginia radio station telephoned the Psychical Research Foundation—a research establishment run by Roll, at that time located in Durham, North Carolina—seeking assistance with what appeared to be a haunting. The manager said the station did not want publicity, but only wanted an end to the "disturbance."

In reconstructing the story, the Psychical Research Foundation investigators—Roll, Teresa Cameron, and Pauline Philips—found that the first glimpse of the figure had occurred on an October evening in 1980, when a station engineer was repairing a door at about 6:30 p.m. The engineer, called William Morrison in the report, was alone in the building except for an announcer in the control room. Morrison said that while moving through the premises on his way to fetch a tool, he saw in the station sales office, about fifty feet from where he stood, the figure of a man wearing a checked brown and tan suit jacket. Morrison remembered no details about the figure except the coat; he did not remember distinguishing a head or legs. This was not truly surprising: The office was dimly lit, Morrison was tired, and he had lost sight in one eye because of glaucoma. The report says Morrison took little notice but could not ignore what happened when he saw the figure again later that evening: It disappeared as he started to approach it. Shaken, the engineer decided to keep the experience to himself.

A day or two later, a young woman who produced commercials for the station reportedly saw the midsection of a man—no head or legs were evident—wearing a brown jacket. From the "slump and the way he held his hands," the apparition reminded her of a former employee, Charles Michaux, who had died in 1978. She was "jolted and frightened" by the experience. When she related the event to her colleagues, Morrison described what he had seen. He said the apparition had reminded him, also, of the deceased Michaux. The next month, a young announcer identified as Jack Sneider reported that while alone in the building one night he thought he saw Morrison, but upon getting a phone call from him realized something was amiss. He searched the building and found nothing. About a month later, Sneider claimed to see a six-foot-tall figure "loom in front" of him but said the image vanished as he ducked to avoid it.

In April of 1981, a young receptionist said her heart "fluttered" when she saw a transparent male figure pass her in the hallway and then disappear. She ran into the back room where some people were eating lunch and screamed, "Oh my God, I saw a ghost!" She described it as wearing a dark suit and said the image shimmered like "heat waves rising from the road." One of those present was Henry Eaton, another engineer, who promptly reported that on that same day he had seen an unknown man sitting in the station manager's office (the station manager was absent that day). The engineer said he had looked away for a moment and when he looked back, the man was gone.

The investigators learned that Charles Michaux had been a friend of the first two percipients but was unknown to the three subsequent ones because they were hired later. Michaux, it turned out, had been abruptly fired just before Christmas in 1977. It had been a highly emotional time not just for Michaux, but for everyone then at the station. Indeed, a violent fight that broke out over the incident at the staff Christmas party had wreaked costly damage on a restaurant. The feelings must have been further intensified by Michaux's death the following year. The investigators weighed the possibility that Michaux, suddenly and deeply offended by his firing, left an "unconscious psychic trace" of himself in the radio station, an obsessive fragment of his personality that lingered in his former environment.

The researchers judged that three of the people who reported seeing the apparition were having emotional difficulties. And three of the percipients had demonstrated psychic sensitivity on previous occasions: Therefore, they "may have been predisposed to apparitional experiences." The information was not taken to mean their stories were unreliable, however, but as a factor that could have contributed to the occurrences. "Perhaps the percipient of an apparition is not a neutral observer," suggested the report, "but evokes an image of a particular person or event that matches the percipient's own emotional state. This does not mean that the apparition is not 'real.' It could still represent a conscious surviving personality, an unconscious psychic trace, or something between these extremes. If there is any substance in these speculations, it seems that the percipients may have responded to Michaux's personality at the time of his firing."

The radio station staff was disturbed by the strange events. But William G. Roll's experience with numerous cases leads him to believe that "many people are happy with their hauntings" because their emotional needs are being satisfied. He says that in other instances, however, the percipients become anxious and "the anxiety feeds the flames," which in turn grow and "become threatening," creating yet more anxiety.

To be sure, this explanation sounds a little like a complex analysis of a simple truth that people have known for eons, long before parapsychologists began trying to explore the mechanics of apparitions and imitative noises: Ghosts can be scary. Consider the experience of a young American minister and his family, who in 1930 moved into a house and, by their account, found a frighteningly malevolent presence there.

The case was described years later by the woman who experienced it, called Esther De Leau in the *Journal of the American Society for Psychical Research,* which published her story. Newly resident in a town identified only as M——, Esther was unhappy with the house her husband had rented, partly because the yard lacked any shade for their three young children in a region where summer temperatures often reached 110 degrees. She was delighted when they found another place, a "big two-storey friendly-looking house, with huge trees all around, a big back porch, and a latticed summerhouse." The Reverend Mr. De Leau, apparently irritated about the move, offered the opinion that within twenty-four hours his wife would find a dozen things wrong with the new house. "So help me," she responded, glaring at him, "I'll never say *one* word about this place no matter what may be wrong with it."

"And I didn't," she recalled much later, "until it almost killed me."

The first indication of trouble came on the day they moved in, when little Ernie De Leau refused to play in a particular bedroom. "I don't *like* that room," Ernie declared to his mother. "There's a goat in that closet." Goat was his word for ghost. Esther told him not to be silly. Although the boy persisted in refusing to enter the room by himself, she did not mention it to his father for fear De Leau would simply dismiss it as one of the complaints she was determined to avoid making.

Within a few weeks, however, in the evening when De Leau was often out on church business—coaching the basketball team, holding prayer meetings, ministering to the ill—his wife began to feel a menacing presence in the house. She sensed that it emanated from an old boarded-over cistern under the summerhouse and came up over the porch roof and into the upstairs hall. "From day to day, and week to week, it grew in intensity and awfulness," she said. "As the evening hours progressed, it grew stronger, until finally, I could time its actual arrival—10 p.m. exactly, it would be in the hall waiting. And as the intensity grew and its animosity grew, the more easily I could 'see' it—a tall, dark, faceless, shrouded presence, utterly evil, utterly vile. Just waiting and hating, there in the hall."

She tried not to give in to fear, "for I knew if I ever did, all was lost." She prayed many times a day and positioned Bibles all over the house but still was not freed from her terror. She abided by her resolve not to mention her feelings to her husband, but sensed that he, too, was aware of the evil presence. She noted that he boarded up the summerhouse on some patently flimsy excuse and was not sleeping any better than she was.

They finally admitted their mutual fear to each other after De Leau had gone off to a three-day church convention, only to feel strangely compelled to turn around almost immediately and drive all night to get home. He arrived at dawn to find his wife huddling terrified with their children in a downstairs room, having placed a Bible on every stairstep leading down from the second floor.

"We then compared notes," Esther De Leau wrote later. "In every point they agreed. There was a *presence*. It was vile, evil, and increasingly threatening and dangerous." The couple decided to move out as soon as they could find alternative accommodations, even if it meant forfeiting a year's rent to break their lease. As it happened, the real-estate company agreed to cancel the lease, and they found another place within days.

The night before they were to leave, De Leau was packing books in his upstairs study, whistling as someone does to keep his courage up in a graveyard at midnight, while his wife waited fearfully below. Then the sound of her husband's footfalls stopped suddenly. "Horror and terror and danger swept through the house all at once like a tide," she later wrote. Next she heard a "crashing rush of feet on the stairs, the door was literally hurled open, and my husband, white and panting, flung into the room. 'My God,' he gasped, 'that damned thing came into the study just now.'"

Whatever the De Leaus were confronting—the spirit of a dead individual, or a reverberating psychic trace from something that once happened in the house, or an entity of real substance that somehow arose from their own minds or reached into their lives from another dimension, or a panic inspired by nothing other than their imaginations, perhaps inflamed by the stress Esther De Leau suffered because of her husband's frequent evening absences—explanations made no difference to them at that instant. As far as they were concerned, they were in a haunted house, they were terrified, and their only recourse was to flee. De Leau waited for dawn's reassuring light before returning upstairs to finish his packing, but then they gathered up their children and left the house—which they had occupied for no more than four months—as quickly as possible. And in subsequent years, no matter where they lived, they always kept a light on at night.

Stepping into the Past

Paranormal researchers have long been fascinated by a rare type of haunting called retrocognition. In cases of retrocognition—a term based on the Latin for *backward knowing*—percipients say they experience past events and environments as if transported back in time.

Reports of such experiences are not new. W. H. W. Sabine, a scholar of the paranormal, suggests that the description of creation in Genesis was based on retrocognition. Cases continue to arise. In 1963, Mrs. Coleen Buterbaugh, a secretary at Nebraska Wesleyan University, said that as she entered a room on campus she was struck by a sudden silence, sensed the presence of an unseen man at a desk, and saw a woman in an old-fashioned dress who then "just faded away." When she looked out the window, the secretary related, "there wasn't one modern thing out there. The street . . . was not even there. That was when I realized that these people were not in my time, but that I was back in their time." As she stepped into a hallway, she said, she reentered the present.

But the most celebrated and sensational of all retrocognitive hauntings first came to public attention in 1911. That year, English school mistresses Anne Moberly *(above right)* and Eleanor Jourdain *(above left)* published a book entitled *An Adventure*. It was their account of an uncanny experience a decade earlier at Versailles, the grand palace near Paris that once was the seat of French kings. Dramatized on the following pages, what these women said they saw there was still being debated more than half a century later.

The Adventure Begins

In the summer of 1901, Eleanor Jourdain invited her new acquaintance Anne Moberly to join her for two weeks of sightseeing in and around Paris. Miss Moberly was the head of a women's residential hall at Oxford University, and Miss Jourdain was considering a job as her assistant. The trip, which was Miss Moberly's first visit to France and Miss Jourdain's second, would allow them to get to know each other.

Despite differences in age and personality, the two women discovered they had much in common. Both were conventional ladies. The fifty-five-year-old Anne Moberly was a shy woman with fierce dark eyes behind a pince-nez straddling a strong nose. She owed her position at Oxford not to her education, which was spotty, nor to her administrative skill, which was deficient, but to her social standing as an Anglican bishop's daughter. Miss Jourdain was capable, outgoing and charming, twenty years Miss Moberly's junior. She, too, had grown up in a clerical household.

On August 10, the women went by train to Versailles. Neither knew much about French history: Miss Moberly admitted that what she did know came less from scholarly works than from novels, and Miss Jourdain's history courses at Oxford had been classical, stopping short of the era in which Versailles had flourished.

They dutifully completed their tour of the palace. The day was unusually fresh and breezy for August, and they decided to walk to the Petit Trianon, one of two smaller palaces on the grounds. The fact that the Petit Trianon's last royal occupant had been the ill-fated queen Marie Antoinette gave it a romantic appeal. She had been deeply attached to the place, which was her retreat from the stifling etiquette and intrigues of the court. With their Baedeker guidebook in hand and, perhaps, a thought of the queen's death by guillotine in mind, the ladies set out.

The cramped handwriting in Anne Moberly's account of the Versailles incident (bottom) contrasts with Eleanor Jourdain's freer style in these never-before-published samples.

41

The First Encounter

Chatting amiably, the Englishwomen strolled through an enormous formal garden and then struck off through a glade. But their directions had been unclear, and they emerged from the woods to find themselves at the wrong building—they had reached the palace called the Grand Trianon. After another look at the guidebook, they started up a lane that appeared to lead toward the Petit Trianon. Miss Moberly noticed a woman shaking a cloth from the window of a building they passed, but to her surprise, Miss Jourdain—who, unlike her guest, was fluent in French and acted as spokeswoman on their outings—did not ask for directions.

The grounds were curiously devoid of other tourists. At a point where three paths branched off from the lane, the women came upon two grave-looking men in green coats and three-cornered hats. They appeared to be gardeners: a wheelbarrow and a spade were at hand. When Miss Jourdain asked which path led to the Petit Trianon, the men answered, but in such a coldly mechanical manner that Miss Jourdain repeated the question, only to receive the same response. Looking about her, she was struck by the old-fashioned clothes of a woman and a girl standing in the doorway of a nearby cottage. Without remarking on them to her companion, she walked on with Miss Moberly, taking the path the men had indicated.

For no apparent reason, Miss Moberly suddenly found herself overtaken by an extraordinary depression. Perhaps too shy to reveal her feelings to so recent an acquaintance, she did not mention her gloom, but it grew more oppressive by the minute. At the same time, Miss Jourdain was assailed by an almost overwhelming sense of loneliness and began to feel like a sleepwalker. She, too, kept silent about the feelings that had descended on her as they pressed on toward the Petit Trianon.

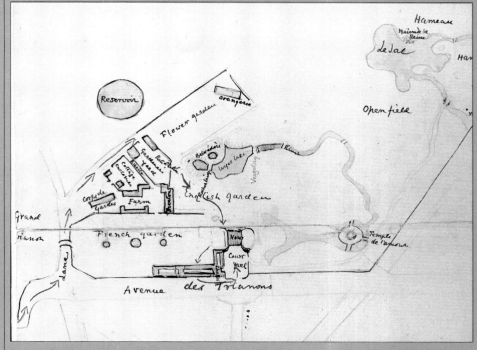

A map drawn by Anne Moberly shows in red the route the ladies took to the Petit Trianon.

The Kiosk in the Woods

In their private, deepening depressions the schoolmistresses followed the path the men in the green coats had indicated until it intersected another path stretching to the left and right. Directly ahead of them, set on rough grass in the shadows of a dense wood, was a small round kiosk, where a cloaked man was seated. The day, which had been so uncharacteristically fresh and breezy, now turned ominous and almost claustrophobic.

Miss Moberly later wrote that everything about her "suddenly looked unnatural, therefore unpleasant; even the trees behind the building seemed to have become flat and lifeless, like a wood worked in tapestry. There were no effects of light and shade, and no wind stirred the trees. It was all intensely still."

The man *(left)* then turned his head and looked toward the women. Miss Jourdain's uneasy feelings sharpened into fear when she saw a look of evil on his swarthy, pock-marked face. At the same time, she was not certain he was really looking at them. For her part, Miss Moberly was thoroughly alarmed by the face, which struck her as repulsive and odious. But she and Miss Jourdain did not express their fears, talking only of whether to take the path to the right or the left.

As if out of nowhere, a handsome gentleman with long dark curls under a wide-brimmed hat, wearing buckle shoes and a cloak, rushed up to the two women, calling out that they should take the path to the right to reach the palace. Then this unexpected guide dashed off and in a moment was out of view.

Surprised at how quickly he had materialized and then disappeared, but thankful for his help, Miss Moberly and Miss Jourdain resumed their walk, which took them through a somber wood. At its edge, the Englishwomen finally caught their first glimpse of the Petit Trianon.

In 1904, Anne Moberly sketched the columned kiosk she had seen three years before.

A Vision in a Garden

The two women stepped from the wood and crossed an English-style garden toward the north facade of the Petit Trianon, which, in Miss Moberly's opinion, looked more like an elegant country house than a royal establishment. Near a terrace that wrapped around the north and west sides of the palace, Miss Moberly observed a woman who appeared to be sketching. Fair-haired and rather pretty, she wore a broad-brimmed white hat and a low-cut dress with a full skirt. A light-colored scarf was draped around her shoulders. A distinctly old-fashioned outfit, Miss Moberly concluded, for a tourist to wear. She felt somehow annoyed by the woman, whom she and Miss Jourdain passed in silence.

Miss Moberly was oppressed by an unnatural stillness and a dreamlike feeling as she and Miss Jourdain reached the terrace and made their way around the palace to a courtyard on the south facade. There they entered and fell in with a merry French wedding party—its members all in proper twentieth-century attire—for a tour of the rooms. The dark mood began to dissipate, and their normal good spirits returned.

Perhaps wishing to repress a troubling experience, the ladies did not talk about their excursion until a week later, when Miss Moberly began a letter to her sister in which she mentioned their search for the Petit Trianon. As she wrote, she found herself once again overtaken by depression. She turned to Miss Jourdain and burst out, "Do you think that the Petit Trianon is haunted?" Miss Jourdain promptly replied, "Yes, I do." They then revealed to each other the emotions they had felt that day and tried to account for the odd behavior and dress of the gentleman they had encountered near the kiosk. After this conversation, they did not return to the subject for the rest of their holiday, and several months were to pass before it surfaced once again.

Records kept by Anne Moberly and Eleanor Jourdain included an annotated postcard of the Petit Trianon. Miss Moberly drew an arrow pointing to the spot where she saw a woman sketching and wrote next to it "Lady sitting here."

Phantom Music on a Winter's Day

Back in Oxford that autumn, Miss Jourdain was shocked when Miss Moberly mentioned a seated woman they had passed in the garden of the Petit Trianon. Miss Jourdain had seen no seated woman. Later, Miss Jourdain learned that August 10, the date of their visit to Versailles, was pivotal in French history, for on that day in 1792 revolutionary forces had arrested the royal family. It had marked the beginning of the end for Marie Antoinette: Ahead lay imprisonment and the guillotine. The women now speculated that they might somehow have tapped into a telepathic trace of the queen's memory lingering near her beloved palace on that black anniversary. It was a fancy that demanded another visit.

Miss Jourdain returned to Paris for the Christmas holidays. On a cold, wet January day, she set off through the Petit Trianon's park for the Hameau, a tiny reproduction of a peasant hamlet, built for Marie Antoinette, who had visited it almost daily. Dreamlike sensations and uncanny perceptions assailed Miss Jourdain as she neared the Hameau. She passed two men in tunics and hooded capes loading sticks into a cart. When she glanced back a moment later, the men had disappeared.

At the Hameau, Miss Jourdain walked from building to building, oppressed by a dreariness that deepened when she paused before the queen's cottage. Reentering the wooded park, she wandered a tangle of paths screened by dense undergrowth. Although she heard the rustling of silk dresses (attire quite foolish for a wet day, she thought) and women talking in French, she saw no one except a grizzled old gardener. Intermittently, faint strains of violin music reached her ears.

Back at the main palace, Miss Jourdain asked if there had been a concert at the Petit Trianon that day. No, she was told, no concert. She began to wonder if she had heard phantom music from the past.

An accomplished amateur musician, Eleanor Jourdain wrote down twelve bars of music she heard at the Petit Trianon. It is reminiscent of eighteenth-century French music.

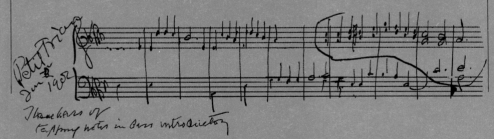

48

A Dead Queen's Living Memory

Eleanor Jourdain's second experience at Versailles strengthened the women's conviction that they had experienced something far from ordinary. In comparing their independently written accounts of the August visit, they were struck by several strange discrepancies. In addition to not seeing the woman sketching in the garden, Miss Jourdain had missed the woman shaking a cloth out a window. On the other hand, Miss Moberly had not noticed the cottage with a woman and girl in the doorway. It was as if they both saw across time, but each imperfectly and differently. Somehow, the women decided, they had passively viewed Marie Antoinette's thoughts. According to their hypothesis, the visions that had enveloped them were scenes from a vivid, melancholy daydream that once had filled the queen's mind. Seeking to link their experience to Marie Antoinette's, they tracked down and studied scores of documents. A map drawn by the queen's architect suggested to them that a cottage had indeed stood where Miss Jourdain had seen one, although the site was now empty. In another instance, an architectural record from 1780 noted a small columned structure that they thought must be the kiosk they had seen.

They were also satisfied that their research had uncovered the identities of the figures they had met. The green-coated men with the wheelbarrow, they decided, were not gardeners but members of the Swiss Guard assigned to protect the king and queen. The man seated at the kiosk was identified as the Comte de Vaudreuil, who had proved himself a false friend to the queen by persuading her to allow the performance of a subtly antiroyalist play. The ladies believed they felt the queen's

When Anne Moberly saw this portrait of Marie Antoinette, it convinced her that the lady she had seen sketching in the garden of the Petit Trianon was the queen.

own displeasure at the sight of Vaudreuil.

Converging bits of information led them to October 5, 1789, as a date relevant to some of the events they observed. According to historical tradition, a messenger had rushed to the Petit Trianon on that day to warn the queen of a revolutionary mob approaching from Paris. The researchers matched the messenger with the man running near the kiosk. And, in a paymaster's logbook, they found that a horse cart had been hired to carry away sticks and branches from the park on that date—the very task Miss Jourdain had seen performed near the Hameau.

All the puzzle pieces appeared to fit. The cloaked men, for instance, seemed to have been dressed for fall rather than a warm August day. Whatever the accuracy of their inferences, Marie Antoinette would have remembered that day with a mixture of nostalgia and sorrow, for according to tradition the royal family left Versailles then

to take up residence in Paris. The queen never saw her beloved Petit Trianon again.

Psychical researcher G. W. Lambert later proposed that Miss Jourdain and Miss Moberly had a genuine retrocognitive experience but got the year wrong. His research indicated that the kiosk and several other key features of their visions were removed around 1774. He suggests that they saw events from around 1770 rather than 1789.

Then again, Miss Moberly and Miss Jourdain may also have seen nothing more than actors in period costumes. Biographer Phillipe Jullian discovered in researching the life of the flamboyant turn-of-the-century poet Robert de Montesquiou that he and his friends often rehearsed historical plays near the Petit Trianon. And Marie Antoinette was one of their favorite characters. In a 1965 book, Jullian suggested that the Englishwomen might have happened upon these amateur theatricals.

Jullian's theory proved influential. Dame Joan Evans, an art historian and longtime friend to whom Miss Moberly and Miss Jourdain willed the copyright of their book, was convinced that Jullian had hit upon the truth, turning a tantalizing tale of retrocognition into nothing but an honest misperception. Acting on her conviction, Dame Joan refused to authorize any further English editions of *An Adventure.* But many who have read the account still fervently believe that the women did, indeed, somehow briefly view a long-dead world.

Royal architect Richard Mique's 1783 map of the Petit Trianon, according to the two Englishwomen, authenticated their visions. They claimed to have seen features that had disappeared or been altered by 1901.

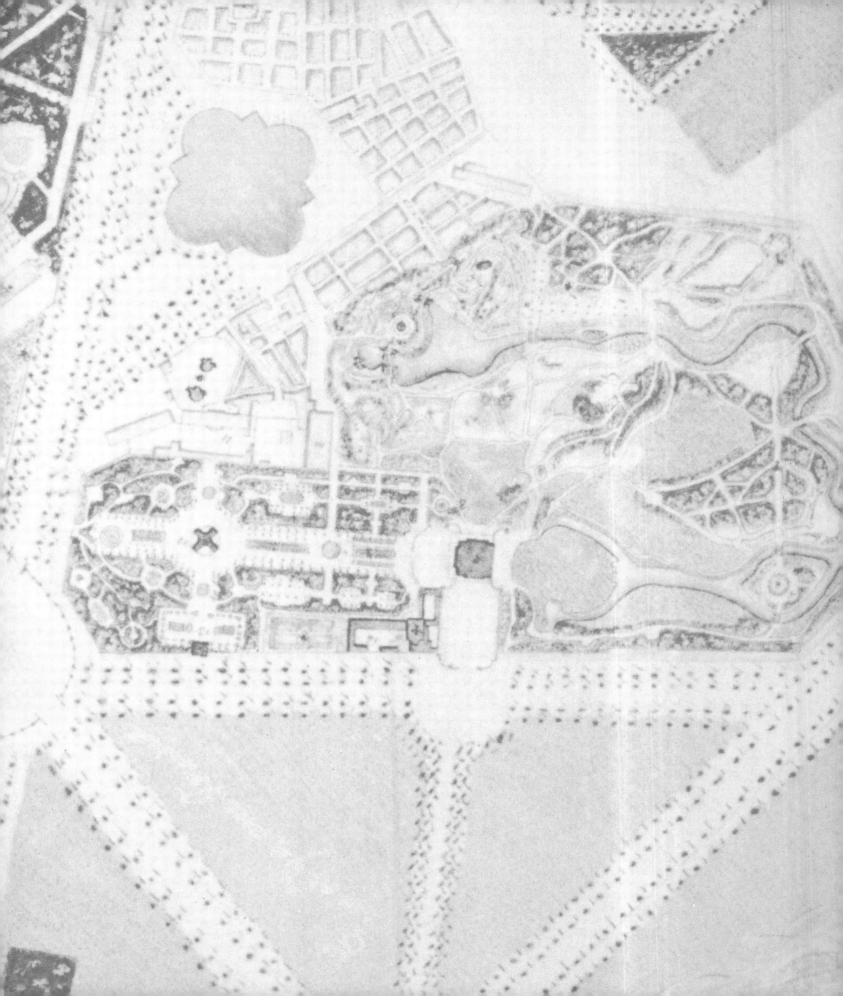

CHAPTER 2

The Poltergeist Riddle

Eager to make a fresh start after her husband's death, Mrs. Frances Freeborn bought a new house in Bakersfield, California, in November of 1981. It was a pleasant-looking three-bedroom house that had been vacant for nearly five years, following the sudden death of its previous owner, Mrs. Meg Lyons. Everything in the house remained exactly as Meg Lyons had left it, from the furniture that was filling the rooms to the clothes that were still neatly folded in the dresser drawers.

Mrs. Freeborn was pleased with her purchase, but as she set about clearing the house to refurnish it with her own belongings, strange things began to happen. On the very day she moved in, she heard loud thumping noises from the direction of the kitchen; because the furnace was on, she attributed the sounds to pipes expanding with the heat. Then, doors and cabinets that she closed before going to bed were inexplicably open in the morning. She enlisted a repairman to see whether the door latches were working properly—they were—and a carpenter to see whether the cabinet was level—it was. Before long, some of the lights in the house began turning on when she was absent. She had three switches replaced, which at first appeared to eliminate the problem, but then other lights started acting up in the same way. She changed those switches as well, but Mrs. Freeborn was annoyed; the man who sold her the house—Luke Cowley, son-in-law of the deceased Meg Lyons—had assured her its wiring was in excellent condition.

About a month after moving in, she began to hang the pictures she had brought with her from her old house. She put up one of her particular favorites—a triptych of three pre-Civil War women, framed so they appeared in three oval cutouts in a single mat—and awoke the next morning to find it neatly propped against the wall below the spot where she had hung it. Naturally enough, she assumed that the frame had simply slipped off its hook and considered herself lucky that the glass had not shattered. She rehung the picture more securely.

The next morning, however, the triple-picture once again was resting against the wall beneath its empty hook. Mrs. Freeborn tried hanging the picture in five different locations but each time discovered that it had mysteriously come down—or had been taken down—during the night. More baffled than frightened, she put the project aside after the fifth attempt.

Ten days later, Mrs. Freeborn found herself seized by a curious impulse. Taking up the picture yet again, she carried it into a spare bedroom and nailed it up in a new spot. "It was as if a presence directed me," she later recalled. "I would never have hung it there myself. It was much too low and too close to the light switch, but I felt myself directed to hang it exactly there. It was like getting feedback from addressing an audience—you know how you sense an audience disagreeing with you or getting into it with you. That's how it was." This time, the picture remained securely in place.

Shortly afterward, Mrs. Freeborn received a visit from Luke Cowley. As he toured the refurbished house, Meg Lyons's son-in-law spotted the troublesome picture and stopped dead in his tracks. Mrs. Freeborn noted his astonishment. At the time, Cowley offered no explanation for his surprise, but he later explained that his mother-in-law had owned a very similar, three-oval picture that she had placed in that exact spot. Since Mrs. Lyons had been not quite five feet tall, the picture had been at eye level for her. According to Cowley, she had been a very dominating and stubborn woman and took great pride in her house and its décor. Indeed, her friends had been known to comment, "This house is Meg!"

Frances Freeborn had never given much credence to what she called psychic stuff. But now she had to wonder: Could the dead Meg Lyons somehow be responsible for the intense feeling of "disagreeableness" Mrs. Freeborn experienced whenever she changed anything about the house?

Because she suffered from a bad back, Frances Freeborn had hired workmen to raise countertops and fixtures that had been installed to accommodate Mrs. Lyons's smaller stature. As the renovation progressed, Mrs. Freeborn sensed a hostility in the atmosphere. "It was as if it—I called it 'it'—disapproved of what I was doing," she said. Still, she did not believe herself to be in any danger.

But as she prepared to redecorate the main bedroom of the house in January 1982, matters came to a swift and terrifying climax. Throughout the day that she bought the paint and wallpaper for the job, she felt the uncomfortable sensation of someone watching her, and that night her sleep was troubled by mysterious banging and crashing noises in distant parts of the house. Rising from bed at about 2:00 a.m., she visited the bathroom adjacent to her bedroom. As she stood over the sink washing her hands, the bathroom window slid open in a deliberate movement. Startled, Mrs. Freeborn feared a burglar was trying to break into the house. Yet, when she peered into the darkness, she saw nothing, except that the screen that made the window inaccessible from outside was intact. Closing the window, she made her way back into the bedroom, where frightened and unable to sleep, she perched on the edge of the bed. Her adventure had only begun.

Suddenly and simultaneously, the bathroom window flew open again and the bedroom window slammed shut with a loud crash. As her dog began barking frantically, Mrs. Freeborn jumped to her feet to see the folding doors of one closet spring open as if of their own accord, while at the same moment the doors of another closet closed noisily without any visible assistance.

One thought took hold in the midst of the chaotic scene: to get out of the house as quickly as possible. Scooping up her dog, Mrs. Freeborn raced from the bedroom. The door to the hall, which had been closed when she went to bed, was now open, even though she had not touched it. Charging through, Mrs. Freeborn felt a strange impact. "There was a zone of pressure," she said, "a mass out in the hall, as if something ominous and ugly was concentrated there." She turned on lights but saw nothing. The dog's barking grew even more frantic.

There in the hallway, two months of weird happenings came to a head. "I realized that I had to get out of the house or I would die," Mrs. Freeborn later insisted. The terrified woman felt three distinct forces—one on either side of her and another blocking her path—forces that did not want to let her pass. Screaming "Get out of my way!" she pushed forward. She sensed that the two presences alongside her were "surprised" when she managed to break through, and the one in front of her fell back in apparent shock. Pausing only long enough to grab a coat and her handbag, she ran out the back door and sped away in her car, still wearing only a nightdress. By morning, she was thinking of selling the house.

The events described in the foregoing account were related in a detailed report prepared by L. Stafford Betty, a faculty member of the Department of Philosophy and Religious Studies at California State College, Bakersfield. (As is usual in such studies, Betty substituted pseudonyms for actual names in order to protect the people involved from publicity.) After considerable investigation stretching more than a year, Betty was satisfied that no fraud was involved in the accounts of "Frances Freeborn" or "Luke Cowley." Betty concluded that some of the phenomena experienced might have been occasioned by physical causes but that many of the happenings could not be so easily explained. "The only explanation that covers *all* the phenomena," he wrote in the *Journal of the Society for Psychical Research* in 1984, "is a paranormal one."

The Bakersfield case appears to fit the strange category of paranormal activity known as poltergeist phenomena. The very term *poltergeist*—from the German words *poltern,* meaning noisy or mischievous, and *Geist,* meaning spirit—

suggests the rambunctious phantom hell-raisers of popular folklore and legend. "The phenomena that have been laid at the door of the poltergeist make up a pretty motley collection," observed Alan Gauld, a psychical investigator and university lecturer in psychology. "The two commonest major classes are perhaps those of percussive sounds—raps, taps, thumps, thuds, crashes, bangs and bombinations—and those of object movements—the tilting, displacement, movement, lifting and hurling of objects."

Poltergeists, then, are quite literally things that go bump—but not usually in the night. Poltergeist phenomena tend to be diurnal—daytime—events, according to parapsychologist William G. Roll, whereas traditional haunting manifestations are frequently nocturnal. And poltergeist activity is usually centered on a particular person, not necessarily a particular place, as is the case with hauntings. But there are exceptions to even these general characteristics. All that can be said with certainty is that poltergeist disturbances begin suddenly and without warning, last anywhere from a few days to a few years, and then typically cease as abruptly and mysteriously as they began.

There is sharp disagreement over what a poltergeist actually is and what forces lie behind its appearances. Even the term *poltergeist* has sparked a lively debate. William G. Roll believes the term is a misnomer, "since it implies an agency apart from any living organism." In Roll's view, poltergeists are not noisy ghosts at all, but are instead powerful "person-centered" phenomena, triggered within the minds or psyches of living, human agents. In other words, what appears to be the handiwork of a restless spirit may actually be traced to the uncontrolled psychokinetic energy of living people—specifically, to what Roll and his colleague J. Gaither Pratt have termed "recurrent spontaneous psychokinesis," RSPK for short.

Most reported cases of poltergeists probably can be accounted for by fraud, hallucination, or purely physical causes. Among modern parapsychologists, RSPK is by far the most widely accepted theory for alleged poltergeist activities that defy those simpler explanations.

Some researchers say, however, that psychokinesis cannot easily explain all the puzzling cases. In the Bakersfield affair, for instance, the only possible living agent would appear to be Frances Freeborn herself. Investigator Betty contends that there was little reason to suppose that Mrs. Freeborn, subconsciously or not, would visit such havoc upon herself. And, indeed, he believes the fact that she was later able to clear her home of the offending poltergeist with the help of spiritual sensitives lends credence to the opposing, "discarnate," view. This theory—shunned by most conservative psychical researchers—suggests that poltergeists are actually more in line with traditional hauntings and have an independent intelligence, separate from any living being.

Gathering data to prove or disprove these theories is difficult, since poltergeist manifestations are extremely rare compared to other haunting phenomena. Roll points out that in a typical year only a few come to the attention of serious investigators. Furthermore, the spontaneous incidents are rarely personally witnessed by a psychical researcher. Investigators generally have to deal with secondhand information provided by observers who happen to be present when the events occur. In the Bakersfield case, for example, critics of Betty's claim for a discarnate agent point out that his argument is founded for the most part on his own faith in the veracity of a single witness, Frances Freeborn—who, say the doubters, might have been hallucinating even if she believed that she was telling the truth.

Interestingly, investigators of one of the earliest recorded cases of poltergeist activity did manage to experience the phenomena firsthand. That case occurred around 1661 at Tidworth, an English village on Salisbury Plain about one hundred miles southwest of London. At the time, the people of Tidworth did not use the term *poltergeist,* of course. They spoke of demons, witches, spirits, phantoms—some of the many names that poltergeists have been called through the centuries. But the trouble they cause has stayed surprisingly consistent, and the Tidworth case is widely recognized as having the classic characteristics of poltergeist activity. In the words of Harry Price, the famous psychical researcher, it "put Poltergeists on the map."

The strange case began when an itinerant drummer named William Drury appeared before Tidworth's justice of the peace, an Oxford-educated scholar named John Mompesson. Drury, who claimed to have been a soldier under Oliver Cromwell, had been taken into custody for allegedly demanding money from local officials under false pretenses. After listening to the testimony, Mompesson ordered the drummer held for trial. Oddly enough, Drury seemed more concerned about his drum, which Mompesson had confiscated, than about the loss of his freedom. The drummer begged for the return of his instrument. Mompesson ignored Drury's entreaties and ordered the drum delivered to his own house. The drummer himself was released after a brief incarceration.

The following month, Mompesson left Tidworth for a brief trip to London. He returned to find his wife and children in a state verging on terror. For several nights running their sleep had been disrupted by loud, persistent noises that had no apparent source. Unseen hands had pounded at the doors of the house, rattled the furniture, and banged at the windows. The members of the household had not known a moment's peace, they told the astonished Mompesson.

The justice of the peace was a quiet and methodical man, not easily given to flights of fancy. He thought the din might have resulted from thieves trying to break into the house. Thus, when the noises returned three nights later, Mompesson took up a pair of pistols and threw open the door. Nothing was there except blackness and a strange, hollow sound.

Loud thumping or drumming noises from an undetermined source troubled the family for the rest of that night and for several nights following, upsetting Mrs. Mompesson so greatly that she took to her bed. Before long the nocturnal manifestations grew even more troublesome. Chairs danced about the rooms of the house, loose objects flew overhead, and chamber pots were emptied into beds. One morning, the air was thick with the acrid smell of sulfur. Things went on in this way for several months. At times, the phenomena would cease for days or weeks, only to resume with even greater vehemence.

In time, news of the strange happenings reached the ears of King Charles II, who dispatched a number of his advisers to report on the weird phenomena. The group was later joined by the famous architect Sir Christopher Wren. Another notable among the investigators was the king's chaplain, Joseph Glanvill, a fellow of the Royal Society. Although nothing in Glanvill's training or beliefs could have prepared him for the incredible occurrences at Tidworth, he brought a keen eye and shrewd intelligence to the mystery, conducting what was in effect one of the earliest psychic investigations.

Glanvill did not have to wait long for his first encounter with the Tidworth poltergeist. On the night he arrived, a maid came downstairs to tell him that the usual annoying bedtime noises had begun in the room of Mompesson's two youngest daughters. The loud sound of scratching could be heard coming from behind their bed. Glanvill hurried to the chamber and thrust his hand behind the bed, but felt nothing. "I had been told that it would imitate noises," the chaplain wrote later, "and made trial by scratching several times upon the sheet." Each time, Glanvill's scratches were answered by an equal number of scratches from the unseen visitor. Both of the "two little modest girls," he dutifully reported, had their hands in plain view at the time. "I searched under and behind the bed and made all the search that possible I could to find if there were any trick, contrivance or common cause." He could find nothing, earthly or otherwise, that might have produced the sounds.

Glanvill's stay at Tidworth was enlivened by one incredible manifestation after another. Flying objects became routine, as did the persistent drumbeat of "spirit" rapping that seemed to accompany every disturbance. One night an urgent knock at his bedroom door woke Glanvill from a deep sleep. Several times the chaplain called out to ask who

Surrounded by a company of demonic imps, a devilish figure representing the Drummer of Tidworth capers in the sky above the home of magistrate John Mompesson, who had once confiscated a vagrant's drum. The illustration is taken from the frontispiece of the royal chaplain Joseph Glanvill's chronicle of his forays into psychic research and reflects the seventeenth-century view of poltergeists as creatures both mischievous and diabolic.

was knocking, but he received no reply. Frustrated, he cried out, "In the name of God! Who is it, and what would you have?" The knocking ceased and Glanvill waited a moment in silence. Then an unfamiliar voice spoke from the other side of the door. "Nothing with you," it said. Later, no one in the household would admit to having been awake.

These events eventually took their toll on the family's nerves. One day, when Mompesson saw a piece of wood moving about in the fireplace, he could take the strain no longer. Firing his pistol into the chimney, Mompesson rushed forward to confront the demon that had so antagonized his family. He drew up short when he reached the fireplace. There on the hearth were several drops of blood.

Soon enough, suspicion in the matter fastened upon William Drury, the vagrant whose drum Mr. Mompesson had confiscated. The drummer unwisely boasted that he

had brought down a curse upon the justice of the peace in Tidworth. "I have plagued him," Drury claimed, "and he shall never be at quiet till he hath made me satisfaction for taking away my drum." The drummer never had his satisfaction. Instead he stood trial for witchcraft and was sent off to a distant confinement. Only then did the strange manifestations at the Mompesson home finally cease.

Was a poltergeist at work in Tidworth, unleashed by the ill will of the affronted drummer? It is impossible to say with any certainty. For his part, Joseph Glanvill came away convinced that some other-than-normal force caused the disturbances. "I confess the passages recited are not so dreadful, tragical and amazing," he wrote in summary, "yet are they never the less true. And they are strange enough to prove themselves effects of some invisible extraordinary agent, and so demonstrate that there are spirits who sometimes sensibly intermeddle in our affairs."

Unlike today's psychical investigators, Glanvill had little with which to compare his experiences, few parallels he could draw with the observations or theories of others. With more background knowledge, he might have focused attention on Mompesson's two daughters, the "little modest girls" who appear to have been at the center of much of the phenomena. Modern psychical researchers suspect that the girls may have had more to do with the events than did the vagrant drummer. In case after case, poltergeist activity seems to involve adolescents. In some instances—perhaps most—they are playing pranks. But in other cases, say some researchers, their involvement may suggest that the teenagers are the sources of powerful and little-understood psychic energies, or even that they actually serve as catalysts, human conduits, through which the forces of the spirit world are channeled.

If Glanvill failed to reach any of these conclusions on

Puritan clergyman Increase Mather wrote accounts of several New England poltergeist hauntings in 1684. He held that they proved the existence of evil spirits.

his own, it was not for lack of effort. He wrote extensively on the subject of hauntings in the years following the Tidworth episode and corresponded with people who had witnessed or heard about similar events. One individual with whom he may have exchanged letters was the American clergyman Increase Mather.

Tradition remembers Increase Mather and his son, the Puritan leader Cotton Mather, as the somewhat fanatical driving forces of the Salem, Massachusetts, witch hunts of 1692. In fact, both men appear to have been quite reasonable and open-minded on the subject of the supernatural. During the witchcraft hysteria, Cotton Mather counseled a cautious approach, exhorting the trial judges to be wary of "spectral evidence" and advising that prayer and fasting might be more effective than punitive legal action in the prosecution of witches.

The Mathers' views may have been shaped by an incident that occurred a decade before the witch hunts, in the New Hampshire home of George Walton. The matter is said to have begun on a Sunday night, June 11, 1682. Having retired for the evening, Walton and his family were abruptly awakened by the sound of large rocks pelting the house from all directions. An investigation of the exterior of the house failed to reveal any human agent for the flurry of stones that continued unabated.

The stone throwing went on sporadically for many days, drawing the attention of neighbors, friends, and the secretary for the province of New Hampshire, Richard Chamberlain. During his visits to the Walton home, Chamberlain himself was struck several times by the mysterious missiles. In his report, he was forced to conclude that the bombardments "must necessarily be done by means extraordinary and praeternatural."

The case greatly impressed Increase Mather, whose own account was published the following year. Like Joseph

Mysterious Missiles

On the morning of November 10, 1962, psychical investigator Raymond Bayless read in the *Los Angeles Times* that a family named Lowe had recently been driven from their Big Bear City, California, home by a four-month-long barrage of rocks and pebbles. The San Bernadino County Sheriff's Department found the case a perplexing mystery, but to Bayless, it had all the earmarks of a poltergeist effect.

Hurling stones is an archetypal poltergeist activity that has been reported around the globe from as early as the ninth century: In AD 858, the little German town of Bingen-on-the-Rhine was pelted with rocks; in 1592, stones weighing as much as twenty pounds apiece rained down on an Oxfordshire, England, farm; in 1903, a Dutchman living in Sumatra was awakened in the middle of the night by rocks falling on him from his bedroom ceiling.

Strangely enough, few of the people involved in these and other such incidents suffered serious injury. The stones almost invariably seemed to float to their targets.

The stones aimed at the Lowe family in 1962 landed in similarly featherlike fashion. The missiles also traveled at an angle—much like driven snow—and many were warm to the touch. To Raymond Bayless, these oddities were all "typical characteristics of poltergeist phenomena." Typical, too, was the plethora of explanatory theories: that the rocks had been catapulted by slingshot or hurled by powerful winds, that they were meteorite showers, that they were produced by underground gases. None of the explanations held up under investigation, however. In the end, the San Bernadino sheriff's office remained as stumped as the French policemen who investigated a similar incident in Paris in 1846. "Whence came these projectiles," wrote one troubled gendarme, "which from their weight and the distance they are hurled, are clearly from no mortal hand?"

Fist-size paving stones bounce off the boarded-up doors and windows of a Paris coal seller's home in 1846, landing at the feet of startled passersby.

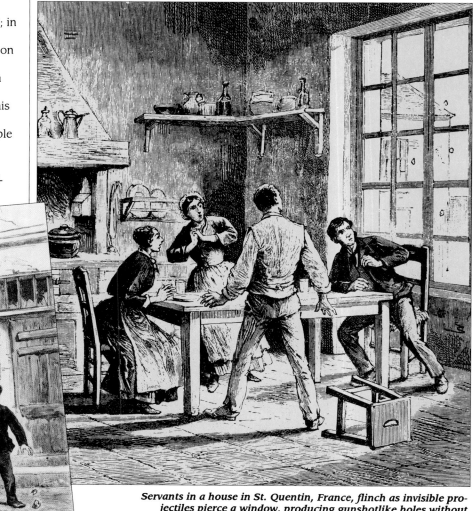

Servants in a house in St. Quentin, France, flinch as invisible projectiles pierce a window, producing gunshotlike holes without cracking the glass. The poltergeist presumed responsible for this 1849 incident vanished when one of the servants was fired.

Glanvill, Mather seized upon the widely publicized affair to persuade skeptics of the reality of the supernatural and to declare his own firm belief in "the real existence of apparitions, spirits and witches."

Mather could not have known that stone throwing—or lithobolia, as it came to be termed—may be a favorite trick of poltergeists, nor would he have even recognized the word *poltergeist.* But his and Glanvill's accounts were among the first tentative steps toward identifying and understanding the phenomena; their work would begin to bear fruit with the Epworth, England, haunting a few years later.

The Epworth case is all the more notable in that it involved the family of John Wesley, the founder of Methodism. In 1717, when the fourteen-year-old John was away at boarding school, he and his older brothers began receiving peculiar accounts of the goings-on at the rectory in Epworth, a Lincolnshire town some fifty miles from the North Sea, where their father, the Reverend Samuel Wesley, lived with their mother and their sisters.

As with the Drummer of Tidworth case some fifty years earlier, the trouble at the Epworth Rectory allegedly began with an unexplained knocking that greatly frightened the entire family. The clergyman's wife was especially disturbed, fearing that the noise might betoken the death of one of her sons. The Wesleys said that, in addition to knocking, they heard phantom footsteps, inexplicable rumblings from the basement and attic, and breaking glass and loud clattering sounds, as if buckets of coins were being dumped on the floor.

The eldest son, Samuel, learning of the events through letters from his family, immediately fired back a series of questions, designed to expose the matter, that would have pleased the most skeptical psychical investigator. "Was there never a new maid, or man, in the house that might play tricks?" he asked in one letter. "Was there nobody above in the garrets when the walking was there? Could not cats, or rats, or dogs be the sprites?"

In each case, however, his questions drew a negative

The poltergeist that bedeviled the Reverend Samuel Wesley's home, Epworth Rectory (left), during the winter of 1716-1717, groaned, rapped, and marched up and down the staircase pictured above. One modern investigator suspected that these manifestations were the work of Wesley's parishioners, who so despised the dogmatic cleric (above, right) that they had already maimed his livestock, flooded his property, and burned his previous residence to the ground.

reply, and the phenomena continued unabated. The Wesleys reported hearing footsteps at all hours, and the rustling of fabric, as though some figure trailing a long nightgown were walking overhead. On one occasion, as Mr. Wesley sat down to his evening meal, his plate of food began dancing gaily about the table. Wesley's wife and daughters claimed to have known the being to take animal forms as well, sometimes appearing as a badger, and other times as a white rabbit.

Although the reported disturbances at the Epworth Rectory lasted only two months, they sparked a controversy that continues to this day. Were the phenomena genuine? Skeptics have claimed that human forces, rather than spirit ones, may have been responsible. Wesley had many enemies in Epworth, some of whom may have staged the frightening events in an attempt to drive him from the village. Some of the servants in the household were thought to be unhappy and may have collaborated with the family's tormenters. At the height of the mystery, Wesley received counsel from all quarters to abandon the haunted rectory, but he defiantly refused.

Others have suggested that the events were engineered by Wesley's nineteen-year-old daughter Hetty, who seemed to be at the center of most of the phenomena. The girl appears to have been highly intelligent and may have found herself bored and dissatisfied with her quiet life in Epworth, and perhaps a little jealous of the accomplishments of her brothers. If it was a deception, however, it was extraordinarily well executed, demonstrating both imagination and technique. Even supporters of this explanation find it difficult to conceive of the methods by which a nineteen-year-old girl, albeit a gifted one, could have managed the clattering coins and dancing dinner plate.

The most imaginative theory was advanced by Joseph Priestley, who would later gain fame as the discoverer of oxygen. After looking into the case, Priestley suggested that although Hetty may have caused the incidents, he believed she had done so unconsciously, without truly understanding the events or willing them to happen. Priestley appears to have been the first person to suggest a connection between poltergeist activity and the unrevealed powers of the human mind.

Priestley's beliefs, which anticipated the poltergeist theories of later investigators such as William G. Roll, were all but forgotten in the storm of controversy that surrounded the notorious Cock Lane episode some forty years later. That case captured the attention of all of London in 1762. And before it ran its course, the tale would involve scandal,

conspiracy, and a suspicion of murder. Once again, a young girl stood squarely at the center.

The affair began when William Kent and his wife, Fanny, came to London and took lodgings on Cock Lane, a short, curving thoroughfare on the fringes of the city. Kent initially took a liking to his new landlord, Richard Parsons—so much so that he not only lent Parsons twelve guineas, a sizable sum for the era, but also entrusted the landlord with his darkest secret. Fanny, Kent confided, was not legally his wife. His true wife, Elizabeth, had died a year earlier in childbirth. Fanny was actually his sister-in-law, who had nursed Elizabeth through her troubled pregnancy. William and Fanny had grown close through the tragedy; however, the laws of the time did not permit a man to marry his deceased wife's sister.

Parsons agreed to keep the secret, and for a time all appeared well in Cock Lane. The first signs of trouble surfaced in the fall of 1759. Mr. Kent had left town to attend a wedding, and Fanny, who was frightened of sleeping alone, asked whether the landlord's daughter, an eleven-year-old named Elizabeth, would spend the night in her room to keep her company. That night a cacophony of bumps, raps, and eerie scratches filled the chamber, preventing Fanny and Elizabeth from getting any sleep. When Elizabeth asked her mother about the noises the following morning, Mrs. Parsons replied that a cobbler next-door sometimes worked all night. That, Elizabeth and Fanny were assured, was the source of the disturbance.

But the frightening noises persisted on the following nights, even when the neighboring cobbler was absent. The situation only worsened when William Kent returned home from his trip and filed suit against his landlord for failing to repay the borrowed money. Parsons reacted spitefully by broadcasting the news that the Kents were not actually married. Not surprisingly, the couple moved out of Cock Lane immediately.

The unhappy business did not end there. Fanny, now six months pregnant, had become frightened that the ghostly happenings in her bedroom were a portent of her own death—perhaps at the hands of the vengeful spirit of her sister. Within a few weeks, Fanny did in fact die. Although a doctor ascribed the tragedy to smallpox, her mortal fright had no doubt contributed.

Matters were scarcely better in Cock Lane, where the poltergeist manifestations reportedly broke out anew in January of 1761, tormenting the Parsonses' daughter, Elizabeth, now thirteen, with noisy rappings and scratchings. In the wake of Fanny Kent's death, Elizabeth became more distraught than ever and began to suffer seizures. Her father, however, refused to acknowledge the idea of a supernatural infestation. Hoping instead that the family was being victimized by a cruel joke, he tore off the wainscoting in Elizabeth's bedroom to expose the source of the noise. He found nothing. Nor did the phenomena cease when Elizabeth changed bedrooms, or even when she slept in the homes of neighbors.

Parsons, at his wit's end, turned to the Reverend John Moore to investigate. Moore, a follower of John Wesley, was acquainted with the strange doings in the Wesley home decades earlier. Believing a similar spirit to be responsible for Elizabeth's trouble, he began conducting a series of séances in the girl's bedroom to gain knowledge of the creature.

These séances gained a curious notoriety throughout London, so that soon the Parsonses' house attained the status of a fashionable salon. Among those who attended were Samuel Johnson, the eminent lexicographer and essayist; Oliver Goldsmith, the noted playwright; and Horace Walpole, the author and historian. Goldsmith, who produced an anonymous pamphlet on the phenomenon, described the theatrical atmosphere of Elizabeth's bedroom: "The reader is to conceive a very small room with a bed in the middle, the girl, at the usual hour of going to bed, is undressed and put in with proper solemnity; the spectators are next introduced who sit looking at each other, suppressing laughter, and wait in silent expectation for the opening of the scene."

Soon, however, there was little to laugh at in Cock Lane. Parsons had come to believe that the ghost of the recently deceased Fanny Kent was responsible for the continued disturbances. Because it made a noise like "a cat's claws scratching over a cane chair," the spirit came to be called Scratching Fanny. Parsons and the Reverend Mr. Moore used a simple code—one tap for yes, two for no—to communicate with the spirit. Through this crude dialogue came a shocking accusation: Fanny, for the spirit now identified herself as such, had been murdered by her ersatz husband, William, by means of arsenic placed in her "pint of purl," a glass of spiced beer. Furthermore, Scratching Fanny continued, she hoped that William would hang for it.

The accusation echoed across London. Kent, now working as a stockbroker, had only learned of the ongoing Cock Lane drama through newspaper accounts. Suddenly he found himself thrust into an unwelcome central role.

People began pointing him out on the streets, and the accusation of being a murderer did little to enhance his professional reputation.

Kent promptly returned to Cock Lane to confront the Parsons family at one of Elizabeth's séances. Hearing the spirit repeat its charge, Kent angrily cried, "Thou art a lying spirit! Thou art not the ghost of my Fanny. She would never have said any such thing." The matter quickly reached a crisis. Because of the gravity of the accusation against Kent, it was insisted that Elizabeth be rigorously tested to rule out the possibility of trickery. Kent's life hung in the balance. If the poltergeist activity was found to be genuine, Kent would certainly be tried on murder charges. If not, then the Parsonses were guilty of staging an elaborate and damaging fraud, perhaps in revenge for the court action Kent had lodged to recover his money.

The tests proved both uncomfortable and rigorous. At one séance, Elizabeth was stretched across a hammock with her arms and legs under tight control. At another, she was instructed to keep her hands in plain view above the covers of her bed. Under the stricter conditions, the phenomena ceased. The unhappy Elizabeth was told that unless she could produce a manifestation of the poltergeist, her father would be imprisoned for fraud. At the very next séance, the child was observed hiding a small piece of wood, which might be used to produce scratching noises, under her dress.

The exposure put an end to the Cock Lane ghost. Parsons was convicted of conspiracy and condemned to confinement in a public pillory, where authorities believed he would be showered with dead cats, rotting food, and other garbage by scornful passersby. The British public, however, remained unconvinced of Parsons's guilt. Instead of garbage, people threw money at the confined landlord.

Many modern psychical researchers share that sympathy toward the Parsonses. Surely, they argue, Elizabeth's cheating can be understood—and perhaps excused—by the fearsome prospect of seeing her father imprisoned, but the fact that she cheated once does not automatically discredit

England's Most Haunted House

The tiny parish of Borley lies in a desolate, sparsely populated area near England's east coast, in the county of Essex near the Suffolk border. It is a somber-looking place, an apt setting for one of the most well-documented and controversial hauntings of modern times—a series of strange events that took place in a dark Victorian mansion that became known as the Most Haunted House in England.

Borley owes its fame chiefly to the irrepressible Harry Price, founder of the National Laboratory for Psychical Research and the most famous ghost hunter of his day. In 1929, Price got wind of peculiar disturbances at Borley Rectory, a large brick house built in 1863 as a residence for the pastors of the parish church. From the beginning, the occupants of the house reportedly had been troubled by ghostly apparitions and strange noises: a headless man and a girl in white, the sounds of a phantom coach outside the house, and the sounds of dragging footsteps and loud rappings inside. And there was the spectral figure of a nun, drifting restlessly through the house and garden, her head bent in sorrow.

Local tradition had a romantic explanation for these emanations. It was said that a monastery once stood on the site and a convent close by, and that in the thirteenth century a monk and a beautiful young novice were apprehended while trying to elope. The monk was hanged and the would-be nun bricked up alive in the walls of her convent. To a seasoned psychical researcher such as Price, this must have seemed a tired old story—spectral nuns and monks, like phantom coaches, are stock figures of the British ghost story. But the Borley phenomena proved to be more complex.

At about the time Price took an interest in Borley, the rectory began to receive the energetic attentions of a poltergeist. Bells rang, lights flashed, and objects flew through the air. Then, in 1930, the Reverend Lionel Foyster and his attractive, much-younger wife, Marianne, moved in, and the supernatural manifestations became more frequent. And a new phenomenon— one that Harry Price considered unique in the annals of the paranormal— manifested itself: Mysterious written messages began to appear on the walls and on scraps of paper scattered through the house.

In 1937—after the rectory had been abandoned as a pastoral residence— Price rented the house for a year and installed a rotating team of observers to document the manifestations. He later wrote two popular books devoted to the case, lectured extensively on it, and discussed it on the radio.

Price's relentless publicizing earned Borley both notoriety and the attention of rival researchers, who would squabble for decades over the mystery. Detractors alleged that the entire case was suspect, scoffing at Price's investigatory techniques and in particular his crew of amateur observers recruited by newspaper advertisements. Critics even suggested that Price fraudulently orchestrated at least some of the alleged poltergeist phenomena. But in the end, the controversial ghost hunter did turn up evidence of a long-ago tragedy that seemed to explain the hauntings—and convinced many that the manifestations were genuine.

Shortly after moving to the rectory, Marianne Foyster found an old envelope with her name written on the back. "What do you want?" she wrote across the flap before replacing the envelope. Later, the pathetic reply (left) appeared beneath her query.

Signs of an Ancient Tragedy

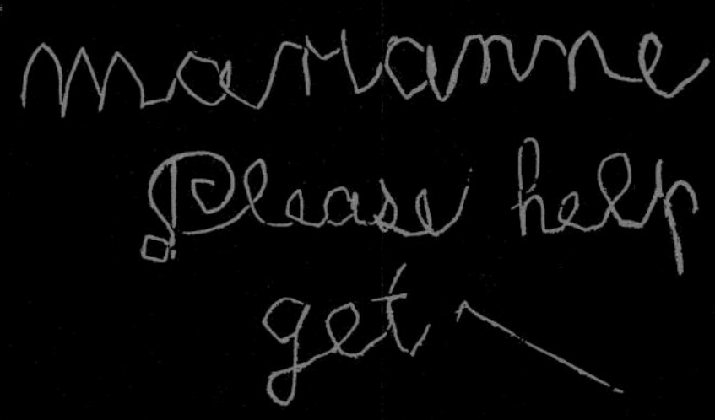

*marianne
please help
get*

The Reverend Henry Dawson Ellis Bull, who became pastor of Borley Church in 1862, was untroubled by the ghost stories told about his parish and did not hesitate to build his new house on the very site most likely to be haunted by the village's restless spirits. Local legend had it that Borley Rectory was constructed atop the ruined foundations of two much-older structures, the manor house of the noble Waldegrave family and an ancient monastery.

Over the years, Bull's servants and his daughters were repeatedly unnerved by strange rappings, phantom footsteps, and the disquieting appearance of wraithlike figures. But the worldly Bull seemed to regard these oddities as a splendid form of entertainment; he even built an airy summerhouse where he and his eldest son, Harry, could enjoy after-dinner cigars and observe the twilight wanderings of the spectral nun.

Harry Bull inherited the rectory, its ghosts, and the job of parson when his father died in 1892, and stayed on until his own death in 1927. But Bull's successor, Rev. Guy Smith, quit the rectory less than a year after moving in, plagued both by the Borley ghosts—which had been joined by the apparent poltergeist—and by the house's deplorable and increasingly dilapidated state. Until then, the ghosts of Borley had

seemed relatively benign. That changed when the Reverend Lionel and Marianne Foyster took up residence in October 1930. The rappings inside the walls became louder and more frantic, furniture was overturned, and doors appeared to lock themselves. More disturbing was the violence that seemed to be directed at Marianne. She was thrown from her bed, repeatedly struck by a bruising unseen hand, and forced to dodge heavy objects that came flying at her day and night.

Harry Price implied in his first book on the Borley case—published in 1940, five years after the Foysters vacated the rectory—that he suspected Marianne of using sleight of hand to engineer at least some of these disturbances. Nonetheless, Price stoutly maintained that at least one of the spirits that had haunted Borley for so many decades had found the rector's wife to be a sympathetic soul. He felt his theory was borne out by the eerie wall writings addressed to Marianne.

The messages, plaintive appeals for help written in a childish hand, seemed to be from another young woman—one who, by her references to prayers, masses, and incense, had been a Catholic. These were important clues that, like parts of a puzzle, would fit snugly into the story Price ultimately pieced together to explain the Borley mystery. It was a chilling tale of murder and betrayal in which the central figure was a young nun, though not the one of local legend.

Marianne and Rev. Lionel Foyster, with two-and-a-half-year-old adopted daughter Adelaide (pictured here with a young visitor), moved into Borley Rectory on October 16, 1930. On that very day, according to the reverend's meticulous diary, a spectral voice was heard calling Marianne's name.

Members of the Henry Bull family play a genteel game of tennis on the rectory lawn in about 1890. To those who visited the house in later years, when the garden had been neglected and the dark brick walls and steep gables had fallen into disrepair, Borley Rectory took on the spooky appearance of a stereotypical haunted house.

This octagonal summerhouse overlooked the "nun's walk" at the edge of Borley's lawn. In the 1940s, an underground stream was discovered to be flowing beneath the path; periodically, dense clouds of small flies swarmed along its course, providing a possible explanation for sightings of the ghostly nun.

Laying a Spirit to Rest

Look under the brick floor in the cellar

During the year that Harry Price leased Borley Rectory, his team of observers uncovered no new phenomena. But a thrilling development of a different kind allegedly provided information that would at last give Price the solution he had been seeking.

The breakthrough came via the planchette, a pencil-equipped device that moves—supposedly guided by spirits—across a board under a sitter's hand, spelling out messages. One alleged spirit, identified as Marie Lairre, related that she had been a nun in seventeenth-century France but had left her order to marry Henry Waldegrave, a member of the wealthy family whose manor house once stood on the site of Borley Rectory. There, her husband later strangled her and hid her remains in the cellar.

This story seemed to dovetail with the most striking Borley phenomena. The restless apparition of the nun and the written messages could now be seen as signs that the nun had been buried in unconsecrated ground and was thus condemned to wander ceaselessly in a vain quest for final peace.

In March of 1938, five months after Marie Lairre's intro- duction, another spirit allegedly promised that the rectory would burn that night and that proof of the nun's murder would be found in the ruins.

Borley Rectory did not burn that night. But eleven months later a new owner, Captain W. H. Gregson, was unpacking books one evening when an oil lamp in the hall was somehow overturned and started a fire. The blaze quickly spread, and Borley Rectory was gutted, at last giving Price an opportunity to seek buried physical proof for his explanation of the haunting.

For a variety of reasons, he did not ask Gregson's permission to excavate until 1943. "Look under the brick floor in the cellar," one of the spirit messages had implored, and after only a day of digging, Price's crew unearthed a few fragile bones that proved to be the remains of a young woman—evidence, Price conclud- ed, that there was indeed some truth to the story of the murdered nun.

A Christian burial for the bones appeared to provide the ghost of Borley Rectory with the rest that it had long sought. No further haunting activity was reported in the ruined build- ing, which was finally demolished in 1944.

Gutted by a fire that broke out on the stroke of midnight, February 27, 1939, the ruined rectory appeared more haunted than ever before. During the blaze, observ- ers claimed to have seen figures moving through the flames; a police constable saw a "woman in grey" cross the courtyard.

Forensic examination revealed that the skull fragments found in the Borley cellar be- longed to a woman about thirty years old. A dentist who studied the relics found signs of a jaw abscess—a possible reason for the pained expression on the ghostly nun's face.

Harry Price stands solemnly on a peaceful spring evening in 1945 as a small cedar casket holding the bones of the woman he believed to be Marie Lairre is laid in the ground by the Reverend A. C. Henning. The remains were buried in the tiny village of Liston, one and a half miles away from ill-starred Borley.

the earlier manifestations. Nor could Elizabeth's smuggled piece of wood account for all of the noises heard in Cock Lane, notably that reported by one sitter of a "large bird flying about the room."

The tale has a chilling footnote. In 1850, almost 100 years after the events in Cock Lane, a man and a boy approached a burial vault in London's Saint John's Church. The illustrator of a book of supernatural phenomena had come to get a look at the notorious Scratching Fanny, whose spirit had been the source of so many wild tales and accusations and who was believed to be buried in the vault. By the light of a lantern, the sexton's young son opened a dusty coffin lid. The face within the casket was that of a handsome young woman. No sign of the smallpox that had supposedly been her fatal illness could be detected. Odder still, the woman, 100 years dead, showed only minimal signs of decay. "The remains," wrote the artist, "were perfectly preserved."

To modern forensic scientists, the discovery suggests an end quite different from smallpox. Slow bodily decay can be a sign of death by arsenic poisoning.

The effects of the Cock Lane episode would be felt for some time by believers and skeptics alike. When a new poltergeist frenzy swept London a mere ten years later, people were quick to suspect deceit. Yet the events that reportedly took place at the home of an elderly widow named Mrs. Golding, in the quiet hamlet of Stockwell, Surrey, proved to be even more baffling—and far more destructive—than those at Cock Lane.

According to reports on the incidents, the Stockwell poltergeist announced itself in a chaos of flying objects in January of 1772. Plates, clocks, and lanterns came crashing to the floor of Mrs. Golding's kitchen, eggs and candlesticks sailed through the air, and water left standing in a pail began boiling unaccountably. Mrs. Golding, a "gentlewoman of unblemished character and reputation," was understandably distressed and brought in several of her friends and neighbors to witness the phenomena for themselves.

It was quickly observed that the manifestations seemed to center on twenty-year-old Ann Robinson, a maid hired by Mrs. Golding only ten days before the poltergeist infestation began. When Ann left the house, the disturbances stopped. When she entered, they began again. Soon after this was discovered, Ann was discharged.

Years later, the maid confessed to a friend that she—not a spirit agent—produced the manifestations, employing clever deceptions and sleight of hand. With the aid of wires and slender horsehairs, she made the crockery pots and dishes appear to fall off the shelves of their own accord. She hurled the eggs when everyone present was looking in another direction. As to the boiling water, she simply slipped in a packet of chemicals that caused the water to bubble. Why had Ann Robinson staged this elaborate hoax? Her confidant says only that "there was a love story connected with the case," suggesting that Ann may have wished to frighten Mrs. Golding away from the house in order to carry on an intrigue with a lover.

The confession would appear to clear up and discredit the briefly sensational Stockwell case, but modern-day investigator Harry Price believed otherwise. Examining the case almost 200 years later, Price observed that "the greatest conjurer living could not produce the Stockwell effects by means of wires, etc., surrounded by people on the lookout for tricks, and in a well-lighted room, without instant detection." If Price's observation is correct, it would prove a strange case in the annals of psychic research—one in which a confession of hoax was itself a hoax.

There would be no such confession of hoax at the resolution of the Stans case of the early 1860s. On the contrary, Melchior Joller, whose family was the victim of the assault, appears to have gained some secret insight into the true nature of poltergeist phenomena but elected to carry it with him to the grave.

Joller, a distinguished Swiss lawyer, arrived one day at his ancestral home in Stans, near Lake Lucerne, to find members of his household cowering in a corner of the fam-

*Swiss lawyer Melchior Joller and his wife, Karoline, (above, with
six of their seven children) were models of sober, middle-class respectability in
August 1862, when their comfortable stone house near Lucerne was
afflicted by a particularly destructive series of poltergeist effects. Although Joller
insisted there must be a rational explanation for the various manifestations,
the disruption of the household and the gossip of scandalized neighbors
drove the family from their home in less than three months.*

ily barn, weeping with sheer terror. Their home had been overrun by a mischievous and destructive sprite, they claimed. Doors had flown open of their own accord, and an apple had flown about the house. Joller, a methodical, even-tempered man, at first refused to credit the accounts, but soon he, too, heard eerie noises in his home and felt taps and brushes against his skin.

The signs grew even more overt as the weeks passed. Soft, melancholy moans filled the house, along with plaintive cries of "Pity me! Pity me!" On a few occasions, family members reportedly caught fleeting glimpses of an apparition, variously described as being whitish, grayish, or dark in color, that floated through the corridors. At other times, their sleep was disturbed by furious pounding noises that came from widely separated parts of the dwelling. As Joller reported in his diary of the affair, "The blows in the different parts of the house followed each other so quickly that, if one wished to suppose the spook admitted human agency, it would have taken at least four or five persons."

As with the Cock Lane case, the Jollers' plight soon attracted the attention of curiosity seekers. When the family became the focus of unwanted scrutiny and gossip, Joller's once-thriving legal practice diminished. By 1862, his property had become so overrun with sightseers that the unhappy lawyer fled with his family to Zurich. Melchior Joller died, bitter and impoverished, a mere three years later at the age of forty-seven.

Although the poltergeist plague had tormented the lawyer, he appears to have made a tenuous peace with the situation near the end of his life. Alone in his new home one night the lawyer underwent one last mysterious experience, the nature of which he would reveal to no one, save to exclaim, "Now I understand!"

"Now I understand" is a claim few people can make

where poltergeist phenomena are concerned. With the founding of England's Society for Psychical Research in 1882, some of the finest minds of the Victorian age grappled with the problem, producing a wide range of theories and opinions, and still more controversy.

Frank Podmore, one of the authors of the society's "Census of Hallucinations," fostered a dispute when he published an article in 1896 claiming that poltergeists simply did not exist. Having examined eleven poltergeist cases randomly selected from the records of the SPR, Podmore advanced a "naughty little girl" theory, suggesting that trickery accounted for nearly all poltergeist manifestations, and that the girls and boys who so often seemed the victims of poltergeists were actually pulling the strings.

Podmore's assertion did not pass unchallenged. The folklorist Andrew Lang returned fire with an opposing view, citing the Tidworth and the Epworth Rectory cases as ones in which trickery seemed unlikely—even by children who were brilliant as well as naughty. "Fraud and hallucination are inadequate to explain all the phenomena," he reasoned.

Perhaps the most interesting theory was that of psychical researcher Hereward Carrington, who was one of the first to seek a biological solution to the puzzle. Writing in 1951, Carrington speculated that the onset of puberty in human beings, combined with other unknown factors, might serve to bring on poltergeist activity. In puberty, Carrington wrote, "an energy seems to be radiated from the body. . . . It would almost seem as though these energies, instead of taking their normal course . . . find this curious method of externalization."

Carrington's ideas would have a significant effect on J. Gaither Pratt and William G. Roll. In 1958, these parapsychologists investigated a famous case in Seaford, Long Island, in which a chaotic series of breakages and soaring objects appeared to center on a twelve-year-old boy. That episode led the two researchers to a sweeping reevaluation of poltergeist activity. If psychokinesis is the ability of the mind to move objects, they reasoned, then might poltergeist phenomena simply be repeated, uncontrolled bursts of psychokinesis? If so, the two theorists continued, then the very word *poltergeist* would be misleading, since it suggests an independent, intelligent phantom creature. It was within this context that Pratt and Roll suggested a more accurate term would be recurrent spontaneous psychokinesis, or RSPK, to describe the process of human beings unwittingly tapping into unpredictable mental powers.

If the ideas of Pratt and Roll are correct, then poltergeists have no independent, or discarnate, existence apart from their human catalysts. In other words, poltergeists are not sprites, ghosts, or phantoms of any kind; they

Psychical researcher William G. Roll, who investigated the case of Jimmy Herrman, holds a "deno meter," a device that measures electromagnetic activity. In 1988, Roll took the apparatus aboard the Queen Mary to see whether a magnetic field could account for reported paranormal phenomena on the retired ocean liner.

are instead simply mental projections of a destructive nature.

But although Roll maintains that "it is generally settled now that poltergeist occurrences represent involuntary, unconscious PK activity," not everyone in the field of psychic research embraces this notion. "Personally I am not happy with this innovation," Alan Gauld noted in the late 1970s. "We do not know sufficient about psychokinesis as investigated in certain sorts of laboratory experiments to say whether or not it has any kinship with poltergeist phenomena. And we must not slip into thinking that because we have applied to the phenomena a scientific-sounding rubric like 'RSPK' we are somehow nearer to explaining them." A decade later, Gauld was even more emphatic in his opposition. "Psychokinesis is only a term for one's ignorance," he said, adding that he prefers the simple description "poltergeist activity" because "we understand what that means."

Gauld's beliefs may stem from a 1967 case he investigated in an East Midlands, England, market town. On the surface, the occurrences seemed fairly routine. A series of loud, unaccountable knocking sounds were found to be plaguing a family's apartment. Some of the thumps were so powerful that they actually burst a nine-inch hole in a plaster wall. Because the disturbances were clearly focused on a twelve-year-old boy, who was given the pseudonym Brian Connolly, the case at first appeared to support the theory of RSPK. But when the Connollys moved out of the apartment, subsequent tenants found themselves bothered by the same loud, violent thumping sounds. Could Brian, the supposed human agent, have been responsible at a distance of several miles? Gauld clearly found the notion unlikely.

Perhaps the most baffling case of modern times is that of the poltergeist who apparently did not want his home turned into a gift shop. The story, which is both comical and bizarre, took place in a 200-year-old New Jersey farmhouse that had been owned by the same family for several generations. In 1978, the house was bought by "Ted Sinclair"—a pseudonym—in partnership with his wife, brother, and sister-in-law. They wanted to enlarge and modernize the building in order to open an eleven-room gift shop. The Sinclairs knew when they bought the house that there had been reports of ghostly activity. One previous owner described catching a fleeting glimpse of an apparition of "a motherly lady with gray hair piled on top of her head and wearing a plain housedress." Another claimed to have been knocked down by an invisible hand, landing so hard that she injured her back.

Unfazed, Ted Sinclair went ahead with his plans, although the prospect of a poltergeist in a gift shop would seem something akin to the metaphorical bull in a china shop. In late 1978, the shop opened its doors for business, complete with separate display rooms for toy trains, candles, greeting cards, and Christmas items.

By then, however, the poltergeist had already made its appearance. A workman found his tool kit, weighing about fifteen pounds, overturned and its contents scattered all over the floor of the room. Another employee was struck on the head by a falling fluorescent light bulb that apparently dislodged itself from its socket, while a part-time bookkeeper was vexed by a file cabinet drawer that kept opening without any evident human assistance. A clock that had not been wound was heard to chime, and music boxes repeatedly switched themselves on for no apparent reason. The shop's electrical equipment seemed especially susceptible: A sewing machine took to operating itself, and an adding machine insisted on printing out row after row of zeros.

Although these events were not particularly threatening, they did cause some annoyance for the Sinclairs. A bur-glar alarm system began going off at all hours of the day and night—whether it had been turned on or not—and had to be replaced three times. The shop's background music system was also known to switch itself on and off according to its own schedule.

On one summer evening, as Ted Sinclair's niece Cindy joked with an employee about the "resident ghost," she decided to call out a challenge to the creature to prove its existence. The results, she reported, were instantaneous: "Upstairs, it sounded like it was on the roof, there was a pounding: one, two, three four; one, two, three, four—it kept pounding. And we just looked at each other, and I yelled out, 'I believe you!' It stopped. It had gone on for 30 to 45 seconds, and as I said that, it stopped."

In July of 1979, Ted Sinclair contacted Karlis Osis, Director of Research for the American Society for Psychical Research. Over the course of three visits to the shop, Osis and a fellow researcher, Donna McCormick, interviewed twenty-four witnesses to the phenomena, gathered extensive background on both the house and its owners, and studied each reported appearance of the poltergeist. Osis's inescapable conclusion was that the case would admit no living agent as the focus of the activity. Instead, the gift shop disturbances appeared to be the work of an independent—possibly deceased—spirit.

What, then, is a poltergeist? Some cases are likely to be the work of a prankster. Others seem to indicate intelligent, discarnate beings, similar to ghosts. And yet other examples lend strong support to the notion of recurrent spontaneous psychokinesis, which suggests that the manifestations occur only in relation to living, human agents. In an essay for the *Journal of the American Society for Psychical Research,* Ian Stevenson, a professor of psychiatry at the University of Virginia, posed the blunt question, "Are poltergeists living or dead?" His conclusion is typical of the debate and uncertainty that seem likely to enshroud poltergeist phenomena for a long time to come: "Neither always," Stevenson wrote. "Some poltergeists are living and others are dead."

Ghosts from Watery Graves

Early one long-ago morning, so the story goes, a ship sailed into a harbor on Brittany's Isle of Batz. Crews of local fishing boats looked up from their nets and recognized the vessel as one manned by neighbors. They heard voices from the ship, giving commands and hailing the shore. Then, to their astonishment, the vessel faded from view, vanishing like a wisp of fog under a hot sun. They later learned that she had gone down miles away at the very time her apparition sailed into port.

Sailors have told such tales of ghost ships since seafaring began. Some of the legendary spectral vessels—the best known being *The Flying Dutchman*—are said to have been sighted repeatedly. Such a ship may prowl one stormy corner of the oceans, haunting the waters where disaster befell her. Another may turn up anywhere as a harbinger of calamity. Others, as at Batz, appear only once—at the moment the distant ship and crew are plunging to a watery grave. In some cases, the ship is not the haunter, but the haunted, an actual vessel known for ghostly phenomena.

Skeptics offer explanations. A real ship, they say, may assume an unearthly appearance when lit by glowing clusters of electricity called St. Elmo's fire. Freak conditions, such as temperature inversions, can bend light so a vessel appears nearby when it is actually below the horizon. And sailors, perhaps because their lives are often in jeopardy, are notoriously predisposed to supernatural views. But some stories of sea hauntings, such as those that follow, persist in defiance of all attempts to explain them away.

A Fiery Specter

Carrying some 300 immigrants to America, the Dutch ship *Palatine* sailed from Amsterdam in 1752. After a brutal, gale-wracked voyage, the vessel came to a calamitous end around Christmastime, off Block Island at the mouth of Long Island Sound. By one account, wreckers used false lights to lure her onto rocks, plundered the ship, and then set her afire. Passengers were taken ashore, but as the blaze consumed the *Palatine* a scream silenced the pillagers. Through the flames and smoke they saw a lone, doomed woman crawling the burning deck.

At Christmastime a year later and in successive years, Block Islanders said they saw the burning *Palatine* return. In 1869, an old man named Benjamin Corydon, who had grown up on the mainland opposite the island, avowed that on eight or nine occasions he had seen the spectral vessel, her "sails all set and ablaze," and that her visits had ceased when the last of the wreckers who lured her to destruction died. But perhaps he spoke too soon: A sighting of the blazing ghost ship was reported as recently as 1969.

The Haunted Giant

The huge, iron-hull liner *Great Eastern*, five times the size of any other ship of her day, was cast in misfortune. Five men were killed during her construction, and another, a riveter, disappeared; rumor said his workmates had accidentally sealed him up in the ship's double hull. As the vessel first churned out to sea in 1859, a boiler burst, killing five crewmen.

Her captain soon complained that he was repeatedly being "rudely awakened by constant hammering" in the ship's bowels—a noise sailors attributed to the ghost of the trapped riveter. The hammering was reported again and again as the *Great Eastern* pursued an ill-starred career. She never sold enough berths to pay her way. Storms and accidents plagued her. In 1862, she struck a submerged rock off New York. Workers repairing the gash were terrified to hear a rapping sound, even though the noise was apparently soon traced to some underwater tackle banging against the hull.

In 1865, the leviathan found work laying transoceanic cable, ignominious toil for a luxury liner. In 1887, her career finished, she was almost wrecked while being towed to a Liverpool scrap yard—reportedly after the legendary hammering was heard again. The ghost that was said to jinx her was finally laid to rest in 1889, when scrap-yard workers cutting into her hull found a human skeleton entombed alongside a bag of rusty tools.

The Phantom Fishermen

One blustery day in 1869, the schooner *Charles Haskell* out of Gloucester, Massachusetts, found a place to anchor for the night among vessels crowding Georges Bank, an Atlantic fishing ground. After nightfall, gales caused the *Haskell* to drag anchor and crash into another fishing boat, which sank so fast with all hands that only later did the *Haskell*'s captain and crew learn she was the *Andrew Jackson,* from Salem.

Later that week, according to the story, a sailor standing the midnight watch on the *Haskell* saw movement on the forward deck. As he looked on, one shadowy figure after another clambered aboard over the ship's rail, oilskins dripping. A phantom crew, presumably the *Jackson*'s men, silently set to work hoisting unseen sails and hauling in ghostly nets. Reportedly, they returned each night until the *Haskell* sailed for home. Back in Gloucester, her crew refused to man her again. After months in port, she was sold to a Nova Scotian who resolved never to sail her to Georges Bank. The spectral fishermen, it was said, never reappeared.

Unexplained Voices On troop-carrier duty in October of 1942, the ocean liner *Queen Mary* was zigzagging to foil enemy submarines when she slammed into an escorting cruiser, HMS *Curaçao*. The mammoth, 84,000-ton ship sliced through the 4,200-ton *Curaçao*, spilling some 300 sailors to their deaths in the icy water.

More than four decades later, when the old liner had long been berthed as a tourist attraction at Long Beach, California, ship carpenter John Smith reported hearing voices and sounds of water when working belowdecks in the bow—the part of the ship that had crashed through the side of the cruiser. Smith said he was unaware of the wartime accident when he first heard the noises.

William G. Roll, the noted parapsychologist, examined the vessel in 1988. In the bow compartment, Roll heard voices he could not account for. A sound-activated tape recorder left there overnight picked up voices and ''a noise suggestive of running water.'' Roll did not conclude he was hearing an apparitional echo of the 1942 disaster but judged the matter worthy of further study.

CHAPTER 3

Horrific Hauntings

One spring night in 1978, a seventeen-year-old English girl joined her boyfriend and a group of other young people in a macabre teenage prank: They walked through a local cemetery, trampling over the graves. Despite her misgivings about the stunt, the girl went along with the crowd, never dreaming that the incident would seemingly come back to haunt her and her family, eventually driving them from their home.

The episodes began quietly enough, not long after that night in the graveyard. Waking in the middle of the night, the girl, identified only as Miss A in the report by an investigator for the Society for Psychical Research, saw what she believed to be an old woman, seated in a chair by her bed. The apparition said nothing and made no menacing moves; it simply sat and stared fixedly at her. Miss A, who was barely awake when she had this nighttime vision, felt that the old woman meant her no harm. She drifted back to sleep and later decided the woman was a figure from a dream.

But this first innocuous encounter with the ghostly vision soon gave way to more frightening incidents. In the weeks that followed, according to Miss A's account, the old woman appeared several times by daylight, following the girl from room to room. Drifting along about nine inches off the floor, the apparition watched the girl silently and froze whenever Miss A turned to face it. Miss A could not see through the figure of the old woman, but neither could she touch it—her hand passed right through the shape.

Miss A, the eldest of four children, did not tell her parents or younger brothers about these experiences. But she began to feel increasing hostility from the apparition, and she grew anxious. One day while the girl was making tea, she felt a force suddenly seize the kettle of boiling water and give it a sharp twist, as if meaning to scald her. Escaping injury herself on that occasion, Miss A soon came to believe that the old woman was influencing her in an evil way. While ironing one day, she felt a sudden impulse to lift the blistering hot iron from the ironing board and burn her baby brother with it as he slept in his bed. Fortunately, she resisted the terrifying urge.

The anxiety of never knowing what could happen next became too much to bear alone, and the girl took her mother into her confidence. At first, the mother discounted Miss A's experiences; later, though, she claimed to see the apparition herself. Looking down the staircase one morning, she saw the old woman drift across the downstairs hall and disappear into an adjacent room. Soon the mother too began to feel a malevolent presence. One morning, she reported, the ghost snatched the vacuum cleaner from her as she was tidying the house and ripped off the cleaning head. On another occasion, she felt the apparition as an invisible force that pushed or pulled against doors she tried to open or close.

The frequency of such incidents escalated, and soon the entire family had encountered strange and sometimes threatening phenomena. Even the girl's father, who had previously dismissed as nonsense his daughter's and his wife's reports, became convinced of a supernatural presence. One night, after loud rapping noises had awakened the entire family, Mr. A spent two hours searching unsuccessfully for the source of the commotion. On another occasion, he discovered water dripping incessantly from the kitchen ceiling. A plumber was brought in, but no leak was ever found.

Miss A's baby brother was too young to describe anything he might have seen or heard, but her two other siblings both witnessed strange events in the house, which they attributed to the haunting. As he lay alone in his darkened bedroom one evening, one of the boys heard loud snores coming from his brother's bed. When he investigated, he found the bed empty and the covers undisturbed. On another night, both boys were watching television with their parents, Miss A, and her boyfriend, when the whole family heard loud noises coming from the girl's bedroom. They raced up the stairs and found that all

the ornaments on Miss A's mantel had been swept off and thrown onto her bed. After this incident, the girl's boyfriend left the house and refused to enter it again.

Finally, a clue came as to the identity of the apparition. One day when Miss A was sitting with her father, she lapsed into a trance and began to speak of an earlier life as the daughter of a French physician living in London in the mid-1800s. It seemed that the old woman who was dogging Miss A and her family had been a member of the Frenchman's household. But Miss A did not explain why this ghost had returned to haunt her. She continued to be plagued by the spirit and soon began displaying other abnormal behavior, purportedly bending the tines of a fork simply by stroking them with her fingers.

Mr. A was understandably disturbed by his daughter's experiences and afraid for her health. He consulted a physician, who ventured a preliminary diagnosis of epilepsy, which was later disproved by a series of electroencephalogram (EEG) tests. Finally, the town's social services department prevailed upon D. F. Lawden, an investigator for the SPR and head of mathematics at the University of Aston in Birmingham, England, to enter the case. He interviewed the family and inspected the house but declared that he could find "no normal explanation for the events reported to me." Lawden suggested to the family that intense mental anxiety, most likely produced by the graveyard incident six months earlier, was the cause of Miss A's experiences. He advised that moving to a new house might alleviate the problem by severing the connection between the girl's daily life and the familiar location of the haunting.

The family was reluctant to leave their home of eleven

years, and the expense of moving was a burden. But six months of living with constant fear had taken its toll. Finally, as they packed their belongings for the move, the apparition of the old woman began to fade from their lives.

Driven by curiosity, the girl returned once to the haunted house. Finding the back door broken, she entered. She opened the front door to admit more light, then tried to use the telephone. Suddenly, she reported later, she felt a horrible choking sensation and a coldness around her throat as if she were being strangled by an icy, invisible hand. She was then hurled through the front door. She never went back again.

This English family's ordeal seems to have incorporated aspects of both poltergeist activity and a haunting: The focus of the bizarre incidents was an adolescent, as is most often the case in reported poltergeist cases, and the action was centered on a particular place, as is usually true of hauntings. That, however, is where the similarity ends between this case and what are considered typical hauntings and poltergeist appearances. In most instances, a haunting apparition, although it may be frightening, is a benign presence that intends no harm to the people it encounters. Similarly, a poltergeist may cause a great deal of commotion, but it usually does so in a playful or teasing manner, with no sign of viciousness or hostility.

There are, however, exceptions to these general rules. A small percentage of poltergeist and haunting reports tell of malevolent, even savage, presences that drive people from their homes, as in the case of the unfortunate family of Miss A. Some reports even accuse poltergeists and apparitions of causing injury or death.

Since the founding of the SPR in 1882, and its American counterpart, the ASPR, in 1885, scores of suspected hauntings and poltergeist activities of this terrifying nature have been thoroughly investigated. Occasionally, the investigators have come to suspect that fraud rather than supernatural evil lies at the root of a particularly horrific haunting. One such deceit, which took place in Amityville, New York, in 1975, received widespread attention and became the subject of several books and films *(pages 100-101)*. Often, though, as in a notable case reported by an English widow in 1943, these terrifying encounters with strange, destructive powers remain unexplained even after the most careful and skeptical examinations.

"There is some evil here, which manifests itself in illnesses, our visitors, recent maids, all seem to get ill and my husband died early in July last. . . . Other manifestations . . . are rappings, alarming noises, . . . unpleasant and inexplicable odours. My sister has twice awakened suddenly with a feeling of hands around her throat trying to strangle her, and a sensation of an evil presence." Thus read the letter sent to the SPR by the distraught widow, identified only as Mrs. Knight. She was describing life in her home in a village called Wareham, located about sixty miles southwest of London. Mrs. Knight, her husband, and her sister had moved to the village three years earlier. Mr. Knight's death was just one of many strange and often tragic happenings his wife attributed to an unseen evil in their home.

The house that had brought so much fear and grief into its occupants' lives was described by G. N. M. Tyrrell, a respected SPR investigator and author of the 1953 book *Apparitions,* as "particularly light and cheerful, . . . the last house one would suspect of being haunted." Built in about 1820, it was a two-story brick structure with a slate roof, located on a pleasant country road. A sturdy iron railing anchored by brick pillars separated the front yard from the sidewalk. But according to Mrs. Knight, these charming looks were deceiving.

Among the incidents reported to Tyrrell were two occasions on which Mrs. Knight's sister Miss Irwin claimed to have been jolted awake by the sensation of being strangled by unseen hands. She also reported feeling an evil presence in the room. The second time this happened, the choking feeling and sense of evil were accompanied by the perception of something invisible scrabbling at the bedclothes. Miss Irwin was certain the incidents were not dreams.

At other times, vile smells permeated various areas of

the house, including the pantry, the hallway, and the bathroom. There, in fact, Mrs. Knight said she was confronted one morning by the odor of decaying flesh. The stench lingered for more than five minutes, she recalled, filling her mind with thoughts of "death and the grave." Mrs. Knight also reported a bathroom light that turned itself on when nobody was near the switch and a portable radio that suddenly gave off an explosive noise "like a pistol shot" and emitted a quantity of smoke, playing normally all the while. It required no repairs.

In 1943, haunting activity in the house was particularly intense and varied. In January of that year, inexplicable noises sounded in different parts of the house on three consecutive days. The first sounds occurred one afternoon as Mrs. Knight rested in bed, nursing a cold. She heard five loud raps in the room, as if someone were knocking on her door or the head of her bed. The raps were loud enough for her husband to hear them downstairs, although her sister, who was in the kitchen at the time, heard nothing. The following night, both Mrs. Knight and her sister heard a loud thump in one of the upstairs rooms, as if someone had fallen out of bed or a number of books had tumbled off a table and crashed to the floor. They searched but were unable to find any physical cause for this noise. The next day, in the kitchen, Mrs. Knight heard what sounded like a heavy basket of laundry being dumped outside the back door. She opened the door and found nothing.

Three months later, Mrs. Knight awoke in the middle of the night to hear a loud thumping noise directly under her bed. It sounded, she said, like "an animal worrying a big bone on bare boards." She turned on the light and peered under the bed. She saw nothing, but the phenomenon continued. She fetched her sister, and they listened as the noise moved to a different part of the room, then stopped. Mrs. Knight and her husband also twice heard mysterious noises downstairs in the drawing room—slashing sounds like a whip striking the outside of the house's front window.

The house was worse than noisy: It seemed to be unhealthy. Mrs. Knight reported that thirteen visitors and servants fell strangely ill under her roof during the three years she lived there. And when her husband died a week after surgery in July 1943, she attributed his death to the evil presence at work. A month later, a visiting sister, Mrs. Fox, fell ill the morning after her arrival. She was racked with pain. Doctors recorded abdominal swelling and inflammations of the mouth and throat, but the cause of her illness was never determined.

Mysterious accidents also occurred. On the very day that the SPR's Tyrrell arrived to investigate the haunting, Miss Irwin fell in the hall and broke her wrist. She said she had slipped on her way to the door, but Tyrrell found only a foot of the floor space uncarpeted, and those floorboards appeared not to be slick at all.

Mrs. Knight and her sister continued to report strange

presences and inexplicable events. On one occasion, Mrs. Knight observed a small oval of light—apparently unconnected with any normal light source—moving along a wall. A few nights later, around midnight, she and her sister saw first a fan of white light near a bedroom door, then a golden pillar next to the wardrobe. The lower half of the pillar was divided by a blue-gray vertical line, as if the light were resolving itself into a two-legged figure. As the two women gazed at this glowing apparition, it suddenly vanished.

About a month later, the two sisters left the house during the day and came home a short while later to find that some unknown force had disturbed one of the brick posts that supported the railing stretching across their front yard. Several bricks were jutting out of the pillar on the side facing the house, and chunks of mortar were strewn about the lawn. A friend who pounded the bricks back into place for the women suggested that a car or truck must have crashed into the railing to cause such damage. However, a careful inspection by Tyrrell revealed that none of the bricks facing the street had been touched and that the paint on both the railings and the pillar was unscratched.

When she first moved in, Mrs. Knight knew nothing about the history of her house. But eventually, when she told her neighbors about the haunting, she learned that previous residents had had similar misfortunes. A woman who had lived in the house had left after her husband's sudden death and her own serious injury in a bicycling accident. Local rumor told of a child who had died in the house with no symptoms of any known disease and of someone else who had fled to a nearby town and drowned himself.

Investigator Tyrrell found Mrs. Knight "a good and accurate witness," who knew nothing of psychic research or of the house's history. Presumably, then, she had formed no bias and had no reason to expect that such menacing happenings would occur. Tyrrell concluded that some of the illnesses, accidents, and deaths that occurred in the house could be put down to chance. The sounds, smells, and visions Mrs. Knight and her sister experienced, however, were "supernormal, hallucinatory or non-physical in character" and provided what Tyrrell felt was good evidence of collective percipience, a phenomenon in which two or more people share the same perception, real or hallucinatory. For their part, Mrs. Knight and Miss Irwin left, to begin anew away from their house's mysterious horrors.

Pervasive feelings of evil and dread of unseen presences seem even more terrible when the victims are children rather than adults. One such experience cast a pall of fear and gloom over the life of a young Welsh girl named Rachel Briggs, a pseudonym given her by Andrew MacKenzie, the respected author on the occult to whom she described her haunted childhood many years later. Rachel and her family had moved in the late 1940s from their home in Wales to an apartment in the English city of Cheltenham. Sometime around 1950, when the girl was five or six years old, she had her first encounter with the malevolent presence that was to steal the happiness of her youth.

She was playing with her spaniel one morning in her bedroom, Rachel recalled years later, when "the atmosphere suddenly turned 'electric' and I turned in terror away from the window to face the interior of the room: Although I saw nothing it was as if I was being gazed at intently and with dislike. The dog rushed from the room and I followed. I ran into the kitchen where my mother was cooking. She asked me what was wrong, but I did not have a clue what had happened and certainly not how to explain it."

This frightening sensation of being watched by some invisible, threatening entity happened again and again, and Rachel began to dread being in the apartment. She dawdled on her way home from school and spent as much time as she could playing out in the yard, where she felt safe. Whenever her parents left her alone at home, she rushed outdoors to escape the presence that she felt sure was trying to "get" her. Bedtime became torture. "I have never forgotten the strength and intensity of this presence," she later wrote about a night when her parents had left her alone to visit with friends. "It was as if a person was penetrating you with a gaze of hate."

Other members of the family also experienced a sinister presence in the apartment. An aunt who came to visit had night fears so intense that she told Rachel's mother there was "something wrong" in the family's home and cut her visit short the next morning, refusing ever to set foot in the Cheltenham apartment again. When Rachel's maternal grandmother, a self-proclaimed spiritual medium with presumably extensive knowledge of the spirit world, paid a visit, she too felt the presence that had been terrorizing her granddaughter. Mrs. Briggs herself experienced the unrevealed, menacing spirit seven different times. And one evening Mr. Briggs felt what he described as an alarming presence lurking behind him as he sat reading by the fire.

Rachel did not discuss her childhood experiences with her parents until three decades later, learning only then that they had shared her sense of a frightening phantasm stalking the apartment. Her mother, who felt that her own childhood had been blighted by *her* mother's interest in the occult, was reluctant to discuss the subject. But she did reveal that in her youth she had shown signs of mediumistic ability and had made a deliberate decision not to get involved with the spirit world. When the family left Cheltenham to live in Malta in the late 1950s, Rachel's mother reported seeing a ghostly Maltese figure who seemed to be desperately searching for something. Mrs. Briggs soon discovered that the building that housed the family's apartment in Malta stood on a site where several homes had been destroyed by wartime bombing.

Such a connection to previous incidents of death or destruction was not found in Cheltenham, however. And when SPR investigator Michael Martyn interviewed a subsequent tenant of the Cheltenham apartment, an elderly woman, he found she had experienced nothing out of the ordinary. Andrew MacKenzie, who corresponded with the adult Rachel until 1983, speculated that Mrs. Brigg's supposed psychic sensitivity may have triggered the terrifying Cheltenham experiences.

That Rachel Briggs never saw her spirit tormentor made her encounters no less terrifying than those in which the spirit materializes or gives other evidence of its presence. Accounts of such fearsome spirit activity span centuries. One compelling example, witnessed by a number of reputedly objective observers, occurred in Scotland in 1695, at Ringcroft, the rural home of a respected mason, Andrew Mackie. Described by friends as "honest, civil, and harmless beyond many of his neighbours," Mackie lived with his wife and children in a small farmhouse that for years had been called haunted. The Mackies found nothing unusual about it, however, until February 1695, when, the story goes, they fell prey to a merciless phantom.

Whatever it was struck with staggering intensity.

England's Churchly Ghosts

In London's Westminster Abbey, the ghostly image of a monk regularly startles night visitors as it glides through the aisles. At Watton Abbey, in Yorkshire, many have reported sighting Elfrida, a former novice nun said to haunt the grounds of this holy place. The so-called Black Canon, Britain's best-documented phantom holy man, is believed to appear often at Bolton Priory near Skipton in North Yorkshire.

Indeed, all of England seems to abound with apparitions, hauntings, and other phenomena related to its stormy religious past.

Those who study such things attribute these mysterious events to Henry VIII's break with the Roman Catholic church in the sixteenth century. The split was followed by the so-called Dissolution, in which the king dissolved the monasteries and nunneries and

took the Church's property. When some of the monks protested—notably, those in Yorkshire and Lincolnshire who led the uprising known as the Pilgrimage of Grace—the king dealt harshly with them. He would, he told the duke of Norfolk, "without pity or circumstance . . . cause all the monks and canons that be in any wise faulty, to be tied up, without further delay or ceremony, to the terrible example of

others." These were the lucky ones. Other resisters were hanged, drawn, and quartered.

Through such measures the ranks of the religious orders were decimated, and church buildings were plundered and converted into private houses or left to decay. Many ghost hunters believe the phantom monks and nuns that reportedly inhabit so many of England's former churches, monasteries, and convents are condemned to haunt the grounds until their old religion has been reestablished.

Churchgoers in York, the picturesque cathedral town in northern England, have claimed to have seen just such a phantom. The city's Holy Trinity Church was once part of a Benedictine priory ordered dissolved by Henry VIII. Legend says the prioress refused to let the king's soldiers enter the convent. She cared little for Henry's Dissolution order and swore death before submission. The soldiers attacked her, and as she lay dying, she vowed to haunt the priory. On many occasions—often on Trinity Sunday—worshipers there have reported seeing a ghost, hooded and robed, gliding through the air about the grounds.

Stones and other objects reportedly flew through the air as if thrown by spirit hands, sometimes striking and injuring observers. The parish minister, Alexander Telfair, was called in to witness the disturbances. He later testified that the spirit "molested me mightily, threw stones and divers other things at me, and beat me several times on the Shoulders and Sides with a great Staff, so that those who were present heard the noise of the Blows." The phantom spared no one, unleashing its violence both day and night. According to Telfair, it spanked the Mackies' children one evening in their beds, and at other times "it would drag People about their House by their Clothes." It even dealt the local miller a crippling blow and hurled a trough and a plowshare at the blacksmith.

Then, as suddenly as it arrived, the spirit fell quiet. But a few days later, like a storm that had gathered strength, the fury was again unleashed. On one occasion the entire house was said to shake as if in an earthquake. Other reported phenomena were also violent: Outbuildings erupted into flames and burned to the ground; during family devotions lumps of burning peat were flung at worshipers, and at times a human shape made out of cloth appeared, whistling and groaning, or crying out "hush, hush."

Convinced the ghost was a demonic presence, Mackie arranged for five ministers to exorcise the house on April 9. The proceedings were disrupted, however, by a hail of stones. Some of the participants, including Telfair, claimed to have been levitated by something grasping their legs or feet; all five clergymen confirmed that report. At first the spirit did not appear cowed by the ministers' efforts, but on Friday, April 26, a disembodied voice announced, "Thou shalt be troubled 'till Tuesday." On the appointed day, an ominous black cloud formed in the corner of the barn, witnessed by a number of the Mackies' neighbors. The cloud grew bigger and bigger until, it is said, it almost filled the structure. The shapeless mass flung mud in the faces of onlookers and, according to Telfair, gripped some of them so tightly "that for five days after they thought they felt those Gripes." Then, true to its word, the specter disappeared.

In 1696, Alexander Telfair wrote an account of the haunting, which was attested to by no fewer than fourteen witnesses, including five ministers and two respected local landowners. At the time there was no means for independent investigation. But modern psychical investigators discount the probability that such a large number of witnesses could have been mistaken in their observations or conspired together to perpetrate such an elaborate hoax.

Attributing mayhem such as the Mackies endured to the work of demons is not unusual in the history of supernatural happenings, and exorcisms or the display of religious medals have long been weapons of choice in the fight against evil. Both these formidable guns were leveled at the menacing spirit said to inhabit a château on the grounds of a medieval French estate in Calvados, in 1875 and 1876.

A family had inherited the château—known in paranormal literature as Calvados Castle—in 1867. That October the owner, referred to as M. de X, had noted several strange incidents, including nocturnal noises. The commotion ceased quickly, however, and all was quiet for eight years. Then, in November 1875, the macabre violence began.

Over a period of three months, M. de X kept a diary detailing the family's travails. He recorded episodes of loud noises, as if someone were pounding on walls and doors, dragging heavy loads across the floors and down the stairs, and battering the house with logs. Books were reportedly hurled off shelves and strewn across the floor, furniture was moved about, and doors and windows flew open without being touched. Witnesses described plaintive cries and piercing shrieks from unseen sources, as well as the footsteps of an invisible entity that strode through the house and raced up and down the stairs as if on legs "deprived of their feet and walking on the stumps." A priest visiting the château said he saw a cupboard rise off the floor and hover in midair. Not a quiet night was passed in those three months. Terrified family members took to bolting their bedroom doors and burning candles throughout the night, but to no avail. They reported that lights were mysteriously extinguished and locked doors flung open by an unseen presence. Bibles in the house were desecrated, and on one occasion, a key was said to fly from its lock to strike its owner.

The family tried to thwart the haunting presence by placing crosses and religious medals on all the doors, but according to the diary, these sacred objects disappeared the next night as a loud noise reverberated through the house. The parish priest conducted an exorcism that seemed to quiet things for a time. The diary related that a few days later, as the lady of the house sat writing a letter, many of the vanished religious charms suddenly materialized in the air and crashed to the desk in front of her. With that, the violence began anew. Eventually despairing of ever being able to live there in peace, the family sold the property.

Reports of the Calvados Castle case were first published in 1893 in the *Annales des Sciences Psychiques*. The editor of that journal, a Dr. Dariex, had examined the daily writings of M. de X, in which the beleaguered man had described his attempts to track the menacing presence— stretching thread across doorways of the house to see if it remained unbroken during the phenomena and checking for tracks in the snow around the castle during the winter months. And many witnesses to the haunting wrote letters attesting to various incidents that supported the diary of M. de X. After considering the evidence, Dr. Dariex concluded, "The honesty and intelligence of the owner of this castle cannot be questioned by anyone."

The evil and destructiveness demonstrated in the Ringcroft and Calvados Castle hauntings were not confined to only one side of the Atlantic. One of history's most savage and relentless poltergeists is said to have wreaked havoc on a prosperous cotton plantation in Tennessee, tormenting the owners, John and Luce Bell, and their nine children for four years. The Bell family haunting, which began in 1817, attracted widespread public interest, and curious throngs flocked to the plantation to experience the supernatural phenomena for themselves. Among the witnesses who came to observe the poltergeist at work was the illustrious military hero Andrew Jackson, a Bell family

friend and later the seventh president of the United States.

According to Richard Bell, who years later wrote a book about the haunting, the Bell Witch (as the force behind the ghostly disruptions was called) first manifested itself as sounds of tapping and scraping at the doors and windows of the family's house. A short time later, noises began inside the house, increasing in both volume and variety. Although the haunting seemed to center on young Elizabeth Bell, who was twelve years old when the disturbances started, all the family members reported strange phenomena. They claimed to hear phantom creatures clawing the floor, gnawing the furniture, and flapping against the ceiling. As Richard recalled, his peace was shattered by the sounds of a raging dogfight or of clattering noises on the roof that suggested a hail of stones; sleep was disturbed by the crash of furniture being overturned and the clank of chains and other heavy objects dragging across the floor. Some of the mysterious noises, such as choking, lip smacking, and gulping sounds, seemed horribly human. Within a year the noise reached such a level of violence that the house fairly trembled on its foundation as if it were under an artillery attack.

More sinister poltergeist phenomena followed the noise. The family reported painful personal assaults. Ten-year-old Richard related how he was jerked awake one night by a pulling at his hair so violent that it felt as if the top of his head were being torn off by an invisible assailant. His screams of pain awakened his brother Joel, and soon their howls of fear and fright were taken up by Elizabeth in her nearby bedroom. From that night on, Elizabeth felt the Bell Witch snatching at her hair whenever she went to bed.

As long as the haunting had been confined to disturbing noises, the Bell family had kept their own counsel, but when attacks on the children began, they took into their confidence James Johnson, a neighbor, close friend, and fellow devout Christian. Johnson attempted to exorcise the Bell Witch by speaking to it in Biblical language, ordering it to depart in the name of Jesus Christ. This remedy seemed to put a halt to the haunting—but only temporarily. Much of the poltergeist's violent activity had come to focus on Elizabeth, and her ghostly tormentor soon resumed its cruel games, yanking her by the hair until she cried and slapping her face hard enough to leave red marks on her cheeks.

To relieve the girl, John Bell and James Johnson enlisted the help of other neighbors. They sent Elizabeth to the house of a family friend, but the Bell Witch, with its assaults and disruptions, apparently followed her.

No one near, it seems, was safe. Neighbor William Porter, who spent a night in the Bell home, reported a physical presence in his bed, pulling away his bedclothes. He jumped up to discover that the cover had rolled up into a bundle on one side of the bed. Convinced that this was his opportunity to capture and destroy the "witch," he grasped the rolled-up bedcover and started across the bedroom to hurl the entire bundle into the fireplace. But he was thwarted: The burden in his arms reportedly became immensely heavy and gave off an odor Porter subsequently described as "the most offensive stench I ever smelled." Overcome by the smell, he dropped the bundle and dashed out into the fresh air. When Porter returned and shook out the bundle, he found it empty—and odorless.

Johnson and other neighbors soon attempted to talk with the Bell Witch. The entity reportedly responded to their questions with a faint whistling sound, gradually progressing to a feeble, whispering voice that was almost impossible to understand. Eventually, Richard Bell recalled, the whisper became clearer, so that it was possible for listeners to understand. "The talking was heard in lighted rooms as in the dark," Bell wrote, "and finally in the day at any hour." Some witnesses suspected Elizabeth of ventriloquism, but a doctor who visited the house on one occasion when the witch spoke put his hand over the girl's mouth and declared himself to be satisfied that she was innocent.

Intrigued by stories of the famous Bell Witch of Tennessee, General Andrew Jackson—shown here in a nineteenth-century portrait—traveled from Nashville in the 1820s in order to witness this phenomenon firsthand. When the future president's wagon was mysteriously immobilized at the Bell farm, Jackson reportedly cried out, "By the eternal, boys! It is the Witch!"

According to witnesses, the voice of the witch grew stronger, and new voices chimed in, some masculine, some feminine, all coarse and abusive. They offered grisly threats and damning local gossip, including accusations of drunkenness and child abuse, among other vices. The witch's voice seemed to take a special delight in trying to break up a romance between the by now teenaged Elizabeth and her intended husband, a young man named Joshua Gardner. In a sweet, gentle whisper, it reportedly urged, "Please, Betsy Bell, don't have Joshua Gardner. Please, Betsy Bell, don't marry Joshua Gardner." In a more menacing mood, it warned one of Elizabeth's brothers that his sister would have no peace or happiness if she went through with the marriage. And when Elizabeth and Joshua were together in

the company of others, it made remarks about them so embarrassing that the girl collapsed in hysterics. Unable to tolerate the witch's taunts, Elizabeth broke off her engagement.

And she began to show physical reactions, falling into faints similar to those observed in trance mediums. Gasping for air, she would lapse into exhausted unconsciousness for thirty to forty minutes at a time. During these stressful episodes, her father complained of stiffness and other odd sensations in his mouth; once, his tongue swelled enough to keep him from eating or speaking for hours. He also developed violent and uncontrollable twitching of his facial muscles, an ailment so severe and long lasting that it forced him to take to his bed. All the while, the voice of the Bell Witch was heard reviling "Old Jack Bell," as it called him, in the most extreme and offensive terms, threatening to hound him to his grave.

Attempts at cures produced grotesque results. A quack doctor gave Elizabeth a particularly vile purgative potion, which brought on what one family friend described as "a copious evacuation of the stomach." Subsequent examination of her vomit found it full of sharp pins and needles. On other occasions, family members found pins protruding, point first, from upholstered chairs and bed pillows.

John Bell fared even worse than his daughter. Still confined to his bed, he failed to awaken one morning. Unable to rouse him, John Bell, Jr., looked in his father's medicine cabinet, where stood a vial of dark liquid in place of the medication prescribed by the family doctor. According to Richard Bell, the witch's voice cried out triumphantly, claiming to have poisoned John with a dose from the strange vial. The doctor was summoned, and he tested the contents of the vial by giving a few drops to the family cat, which promptly fell dead, whereupon the doctor threw the remains of the unknown concoction into the fire. John Bell was pronounced dead the following morning. Apparently

not content to let him rest in peace, the witch was said to have disrupted Bell's funeral by singing coarse songs.

With John Bell's death, the haunting appeared to have run its course. Little was seen or heard of the witch until several months later, when an object resembling a cannonball purportedly plummeted down the chimney one evening and exploded in a puff of smoke. A voice allegedly called out, "I'm going, and will be gone for seven years." True to this prophecy, the hauntings ceased, and a few manifestations recurred seven years later. By then Elizabeth had married and moved away, and the only occupants of the house were the widowed Luce Bell and two of her sons. This time, however, the events were mild—some scratching sounds and tugging of bedclothes—and lasted only two weeks. Before vanishing at the end of this period, the witch promised to return in 107 years. The date appointed for its return arrived in 1935 but, fortunately, nothing happened.

In his 1846 diary of the affair, titled *Our Family Trouble*, Richard Bell concluded that from the start the witch seemed to have two purposes. "One was the persecution of Father to the end of his life. The other, the vile purpose of destroying the anticipated happiness that thrilled the heart of Betsy." In examining the case many years later, noted Hungarian psychoanalyst and psychical researcher Nandor Fodor concluded that the witch was not a spirit or ghost of the dead returned to haunt the Bells. He suggested instead that "the Witch came into manifested life through Betsy Bell." That is, according to Fodor, it was a splinter of Eliza-

The House of the Faces

As she walked into her modest kitchen on a sultry August morning in 1971, Maria Gomez Pereira *(left),* a Spanish housewife, was startled by what appeared to be the likeness of a face painted on her cement floor. Was she dreaming or perhaps hallucinating, she wondered? No, this strange image that now spotted her floor did indeed look like the beginning of a painting—a color portrait.

As the days passed, the image became more detailed, and news of the mysterious face spread quickly through the tiny village of Belmez, near Cordoba in southern Spain. Alarmed by the inexplicable image and disturbed by the growing numbers of sightseers, the Pereiras decided to destroy the face; six days after it appeared, Maria's son Miguel took a sledgehammer to the floor. A new floor was laid and the Pereiras' lives returned to normal.

But not for long. Within a week a new face began to appear in the same place as the old one. This face, apparently that of a middle-aged man, was even more detailed. First the eyes appeared, then the nose, lips, and chin.

Now there was no way to keep the curious away. Hundreds of people lined up outside of the house each day, clamoring to see what had come to be known as the House of the Faces. The police had to be called in to control the crowds. As news of the event spread, it was decided that the image should be preserved. It was carefully cut from the floor, mounted behind glass, and hung beside the Pereiras' fireplace.

Before the floor was repaired, investigators excavated the spot and found a number of human bones nine feet underground. Some concluded that the faces that had appeared on the floor were those of the deceased. Others were not satisfied with this explanation, for it was well known that most of the houses on the street had been built over a former graveyard—yet only the Pereira home had been afflicted with mysterious faces.

Two weeks after the kitchen floor had been repaired again, another image appeared. A fourth—a female face—followed two weeks later. Around this face there appeared numerous smaller ones; observers counted anywhere from nine to eighteen.

Over the years the faces changed shape and some faded away. And in the early 1980s, more began to appear.

What—or who—created the ghostly faces on this humble cottage floor? At least one researcher has hinted that the images were the work of a Pereira family member playing a joke that got out of hand. But some chemists who examined the cement reported that they were baffled by the phenomenon. Scientists, university professors, parapsychologists, the police, priests, and others have painstakingly investigated the images on Maria Gomez Pereira's kitchen floor, but they have not explained beyond doubt how the visages got there.

Among the striking portraits that have appeared on the floor of Maria Pereira's modest kitchen are the images of an elderly couple (top); a bearded old man wearing a shawl; a dark-haired woman clasping a goblet; and an expressionistic portrait of a man (bottom), which was eventually cut out of the cement floor and then mounted.

While Esther Cox lived in this Amherst, Nova Scotia, house in the late 1870s, she seemed to be the victim of a malevolent spirit that flung knives through the air, set fires, smashed furniture, and finally forced her to flee.

beth's own personality, formed at the onset of puberty, and developing into an independent entity.

Fodor theorized that the psychological shock of entering adolescence sometimes triggers the release of repressed traumatic memories. He speculated that the witch's—Elizabeth's—persecution of John Bell and the castigation inflicted on herself stemmed from the father's sexual abuse of his daughter at a young age. Yet, Fodor goes on to admit, "no psychologist would credit split personalities with manifestations and powers outside the range of the body"—such as those demonstrated by the Bell Witch. "Obviously, we are dealing with facts for which we have no adequate theories within normal or abnormal psychology."

In 1878 and 1879, half a century after the final appearance of the Bell Witch, a rented cottage in the Canadian town of Amherst, Nova Scotia, became the scene of a poltergeist haunting as horrible as that in Tennessee. In Amherst, the central figure was nineteen-year-old Esther Cox, who lived with her siblings Jennie and William in the home of their married sister Olive Teed, and Olive's husband, Daniel, a

foreman at a shoe factory. The Teeds' two young children and Daniel's brother John completed this extended family.

As set out in the 1888 book *The Great Amherst Mystery,* written by Walter Hubbell, an itinerant actor, sometime boarder at the Teed house, and eyewitness to the episode, the strange events began one night as Esther and Jennie, who shared a bed, were preparing to go to sleep. Esther suddenly leaped up, screaming that there was a mouse in the bed. The girls searched the bedclothes; although they found nothing, they said they saw the mattress moving as if something were stirring in its interior. The following night, both Esther and Jennie heard a noise that seemed to come from a box of fabric scraps under the bed. Pulling the box out into the room, they were astonished to see it jump about a foot into the air and land on its side. As quickly as they righted it, they claimed, the box jumped again. The sisters' screams awakened Daniel Teed; he saw nothing unusual and sent the girls back to bed.

It was on the third night that Daniel and other members of the household finally found cause to believe in Esther and Jennie. On this night, Esther went to bed early, complaining of a fever. Jennie joined her in bed at about ten p.m. A few minutes later, Esther tore off the bedclothes and sprang into the middle of the room, crying out in terror, "My God! What is happening to me? I'm dying!" Lighting the lamp, Jennie saw her sister's face flushed fiery red, her eyes bulging, and her hair practically standing on end.

Jennie's screams brought the other adults in the house running. They watched in amazement as Esther's face changed color from bright red to ghostly white. As Jennie and Olive helped Esther back to bed, her screaming gave way to choking and gasping, and she forced out the words "I am swelling up and shall certainly burst!" Everyone in the room could see that her body was indeed swelling. She was also hot to the touch and alternated between grinding her teeth ferociously and wailing with pain. Suddenly an explosive sound, like a clap of thunder, filled the room. As three more loud reports, seeming to originate from under the bed, reverberated through the room, Esther's swelling subsided as quickly as it had come on. She then sank into a slumber so deep her family feared at first that she was dead.

According to Hubbell, four nights later the mysterious, tormenting force struck Esther once more. The painful swelling and screaming were repeated, and several members of the household claimed to see Esther's pillow and bedclothes fly through the air, hurled by invisible hands. As before, a series of shatteringly loud explosions signaled the end of the attack and the return of Esther's body to normal.

Daniel Teed decided that the time had come to consult a doctor on behalf of his sister-in-law. A local physician, Dr. Carritte, attended the girl on the following night and reported his astonishment as he watched Esther's pillow slide back and forth beneath her head and heard bursts of noise from under her bed. Dr. Carritte searched but found no source for the loud reports. He then claimed to witness the most terrifying manifestations to occur since the start of the haunting: Esther's bedclothes flew from her bed, and a loud scratching noise was heard as letters nearly a foot high appeared on a bedroom wall, as if carved into the plaster by a dull metal spike. The message spelled out by the

savage spirit read "Esther Cox, you are mine to kill." Next, a chunk of plaster tore loose from the wall and hurled itself across the room to land at Dr. Carritte's feet, and the room shook from thunderous pounding on the walls. After two hours of such commotion, calm descended.

On the following day, the doctor returned to find other bizarre activities. He said potatoes flew through the air, narrowly missing him and Esther. No sooner had he given the troubled girl a dose of sedative, he recalled, than he heard the same pounding that had filled her bedroom the previous night. The sound next seemed to move out of the house and turn into a vigorous thumping on the roof. When he stepped out to observe the roof he saw nothing, although the sound, audible two hundred yards away, resembled the noise of a sledgehammer smashing against the shingles.

In the days that followed, the haunting of Esther became increasingly destructive. Fires broke out in various parts of the house. Lighted matches materialized in midair

Amityville: Horror or Hoax?

Ronald DeFeo, Jr., the eldest son of an Amityville, New York, auto dealer, claimed the devil made him do it. On a November night in 1974, DeFeo murdered his parents and four brothers and sisters. Despite an insanity plea, he was charged and convicted on six counts of second-degree murder.

With DeFeo behind bars, the family home was put up for sale. Kathy and George Lutz, a young couple from nearby Syosset, fell in love with the three-story Dutch colonial. Even when they learned the house had been the scene of a grisly crime, they were not dissuaded. On December 18, 1975, the Lutzes and their children moved into 112 Ocean Avenue.

Almost immediately, the Lutzes would later claim, the family felt "unseen forces" in the house. An eerie rapping seemed to come from nowhere. Locked windows and doors mysteriously opened. A priest who agreed to bless the house was met by a disembodied voice that yelled "get out!"

The bizarre events intensified. Kathy Lutz claimed to have levitated above her bed and been beaten by an invisible intruder. A horrific green slime dripped from a ceiling. Finally, just twenty-eight days after moving in, the Lutzes fled in terror from their home.

Soon afterward, the couple teamed up with writer Jay Anson to produce the bestseller about their supposed nightmare, *The Amityville Horror*. A successful movie followed. Although the book was labeled "A True Story," most experts scoffed. Psychical researchers doubted the story, citing inconsistencies and distortions. Most damaging was a claim from DeFeo's lawyer, William Weber. He and the Lutzes, he said, had discussed the murder case and the Lutz family's alleged supernatural experiences in connection with a book Weber was to write. Weber labeled the horror story a hoax created "over many bottles of wine."

The scene of a grisly multiple murder in 1974, this attractive house in Amityville, New York, gained further notoriety after George and Kathy Lutz (left) moved in and claimed they were terrorized by supernatural forces. Their controversial story—disputed by many—was retold in the book The Amityville Horror and the film of the same name.

and dropped onto the beds. Knives and forks flew through the air and stuck quivering in the woodwork. A heavy glass paperweight hurtled across the living room, striking the sofa a few inches from a visitor's head. Pieces of furniture suddenly overturned or smashed violently into the walls.

And Esther continued to bear the brunt of the poltergeist's hostility. Other members of the household reported loud slaps and saw vivid red finger marks appear on Esther's face—the signs, they thought, of beatings by phantom hands. Quantities of straight pins appeared and thrust themselves into her face and body. On one occasion, some unknown force wrenched a pocketknife from the hand of a neighborhood boy and stabbed it into Esther's back.

To escape the vicious presence, Esther began to board with neighbors. To no avail, it seemed. By all accounts, the poltergeist followed her and attacked her wherever she went, and in the end, she had to go home. By July 1879—less than a year after it began—the haunting had become so destructive that the Teeds' landlord asked the family to leave. Rather than uproot everyone, Esther left home again.

The young woman had found work on a farm. But when the farmer's barn caught fire and burned down, Esther was convicted of arson and sentenced to four months' imprisonment. Perhaps if there was an unknown power haunting the young woman, it was satisfied by the infliction of this blow. Esther was released from jail after serving one month of her sentence and by all reports seems to have led a normal, uneventful life thereafter, unmolested by the mysterious forces that had for so long destroyed her peace.

In describing Esther Cox's case to a colleague in 1883, Dr. Carritte wrote: "Honestly skeptical persons were on all occasions soon convinced that there was no fraud or deception in the case. It would take me an entire week to write you a full history of my connection with those strange doings. Were I to publish the case in the medical journals, as you suggest, I doubt if it would be believed by physicians generally. I am certain I could not have believed such apparent miracles had I not witnessed them."

Reports of horrifying apparitions and poltergeist activity are by no means confined to ages gone by. And the phenomena exhibited in such past cases are strikingly similar to those that have occurred more recently, despite the fact that generations, even centuries, may separate them. A full hundred years after the haunting of Esther Cox, for example, a New England family endured the first in a series of frightening visitations that would terrorize their home intermittently for more than two years.

Factory worker Joe Berini (a pseudonym assigned by parapsychologists investigating the case) and his wife, Rose, lived with Rose's two children by a previous marriage, John and Daisy, in the house where Joe's father had grown up—a house where several members of the father's family had died. Rose, who suffered the most physically and emotionally from the malevolent force that attacked the Berini home, was the first person to witness anything unusual in the house.

One night in May 1979, Rose said, she heard a little girl's voice crying "Mama, Mama, this is Serena." (Later investigations disclosed that Joe's father had had a sister named Serena who had died in the house more than half a century before, at the age of five.) The mysterious voice in the night seemed to have been a veiled portent of impending disaster. Daisy, who was nine at the time, was scheduled for a tonsillectomy the next day. The little girl went into cardiac arrest under the anesthetic, and she nearly died on the operating table.

This was the first of several occasions on which the voice claiming to be Serena allegedly spoke to the Berinis at a time of a family medical crisis. The voice was heard the next month, on the night before Joe's grandmother suffered a stroke, and again in November on the night before the old woman's death. Another time, Joe was awakened by the little girl's voice and found Rose choking in her sleep. Rose said later that she had been dreaming that her first husband was strangling her. In all, Rose and Joe claimed to hear the Serena voice in the night half a dozen times.

According to investigators' reports, from November

1979 until March 1981, life in the Berini house returned to normal. Then the strange events resumed and quickly escalated in horror and intensity. The second round of the haunting began when Rose saw the figure of a young boy, dressed all in white, walking along the upstairs hall in the middle of the night. This apparition returned for a second visit a week and a half later, and this time Rose heard the boy ask, in what she described as a sweet voice, "Where do all the lonely people go? Where do I belong?"

A few nights later, Joe saw the apparition, too, and heard it declare that a lie had been told, but the truth would come out. He said he saw the small, white-clad figure visit each of the three bedrooms in the house and also saw it kneel in the hallway as if attempting to lift the rug. When Joe took up the rug and floorboards at that spot, he found a religious medal with a broken chain, obviously an old one. Joe wondered if the boy in white might be the ghost of his uncle Giorgio, who had died near the house at the age of eight, some years after the death of little Serena. Inquiries among family and friends turned up the fact that Giorgio had been buried in his white First Communion suit.

The Giorgio apparition began appearing to the Berinis more frequently, two or three times a week. Sometimes, they claimed, it would give brief answers to questions. At other times it would make accusations about Giorgio's twin brother, Carlos, who had survived into adulthood and was living nearby with his wife and children. Joe asked his uncle Carlos to explain the apparition's remarks about something—no one knew what—that had been taken from the house, but Carlos professed not to know what the boy in white might mean. One night the apparition announced, "My oldest brother is the only one who can help me," which Joe took to mean that Giorgio's ghost had been mistaking Joe for his father. When the apparition left that night, the telephone next to Rose and Joe's bed jumped off its table and flew across the room. After this apparent poltergeist activity had repeated itself more than a dozen times, Joe tried to telephone his parents' home to warn them to expect a visit from the Giorgio apparition, but each time he mentioned his late uncle's name, he said, the line went dead.

On advice from a local priest, the Berinis decided to ignore the apparition if it appeared again. When Rose paid no attention to the figure in white on its next visit, the closet door in her bedroom began opening and slamming repeatedly with no apparent physical cause. A few days later, Rose and Joe claimed to hear footsteps running on the stairs at a time when their children were out of the house. Later that same day, Rose claimed, an invisible force pulled a box of macaroni out of her hands while she was cooking dinner and spilled the contents on the floor. Since ignoring the apparition had not worked, the Berinis again sought their church's help. The following evening, two priests came to the house and celebrated Mass. They anointed the house with holy oil and blessed every room with incense and holy water. The apparition allegedly returned the next night but left when Joe commanded it in the name of Christ, as a priest had suggested. In a matter of hours the figure reappeared, but its visits became less frequent thereafter.

Unhappily for the Berinis, the gradual disappearance of the phantom Giorgio was accompanied by the coming of another, more menacing, figure. This new apparition, described as a hunchbacked male figure in a black cape, made its initial appearance in June 1981 and returned regularly throughout the summer. Notable for its large feet and gruff voice, this fearsome apparition refused to identify itself, apart from a sarcastic claim that it was "a minister of God." It often appeared when Rose was saying her rosary, she recalled, and seemed bent on distracting her from her prayers with obscenities.

Poltergeist activity in the house reportedly increased in violence as the black-clad apparition became a regular visitor. Rose, Joe, and their fifteen-year-old son, John, all claimed to have been struck by flying objects, with Rose bearing the brunt of the attacks. The telephone in Rose and Joe's bedroom continued flying about the room, and a bedside lamp repeatedly fell over and struck Rose on the head. Perfume bottles fell from the dresser to the bedroom floor, and furniture in several rooms was overturned or moved about by unseen hands. Religious objects came in for especially malicious attention from the poltergeist, as figurines were broken and crucifixes removed from the walls. Dishes soared through the air to strike members of the family. The door of the freezer flew open and hit Rose in the head, and the retractable attic staircase banged open and shut, cracking the hallway ceiling with the force of its movement and violently striking Rose on one occasion.

The family said that Rose was the victim of unseen assailants, too, which acted without benefit of household objects. One evening during dinner, her arm was suddenly twisted behind her back and her head was wrenched to one side with such violence that she choked and turned blue. She recovered only when her husband rushed her outside to get some fresh air. On several different occasions, Joe claimed, he saw his wife being pulled out of bed as she slept, suspended in the air, then dropped with a crash to the floor. After one of these incidents, Rose found marks on her arms and legs, as if she had been gripped with bruising force. Three times she claimed to be scratched by an unseen assailant who made her feel that her flesh was burning. Bleeding gouges marked her chest, and an upside-down cross was scratched on her back.

The hunchbacked figure supposedly launched its most violent attack in early August, two months after its first appearance. Shortly after Joe left for night-shift work in the factory, as Rose later recalled the incident, "the walls started to bang . . . and the bed was raising off the floor. I tried to scream and the door slammed so I could not get out of the room. The dog was growling and the door opened." As she ran screaming into the hall, the doors to the children's rooms slammed shut; she was dragged inexorably back into her own bedroom. There, unseen hands choked and scratched her, and she seized the telephone to call Joe. He rushed home to find the bed leaping as high as two feet in the air and Rose huddled in a corner, tightly clutching a crucifix and a bottle of holy water.

Rose and Joe chose to remain in their home even after this night of terror, but a few weeks later, when they awoke one morning to find a heavy carving knife plunged into the kitchen table, they decided that the time had come to try a full-scale exorcism of the house. The family moved out for a month, storing their furnishings in the garage. A priest performed the complex rite in the empty house in September, and the Berinis moved back in and took up their life. The Serena voice, the Giorgio figure, and the sinister, black-caped "minister of God" did not return to haunt them.

About a month after the incidents had ceased, William G. Roll and Steven Tringale of the Psychical Research Foundation in Durham, North Carolina, investigated the case. A number of the Berinis' friends and neighbors, including their priest, claimed to have witnessed various poltergeist incidents at the family's home and attested to their authenticity. Since Rose seemed to be the focus of much of the activity, she was given a test to determine how fantasy prone she might be; she scored very low. Joe Berini also took the test, on which he scored slightly higher than Rose, suggesting, according to the investigators, that his experiences were perhaps triggered by his wife's.

As in so many instances of hauntings and poltergeist activity, however, the investigators found the case very complex. Rose Berini exhibited a number of psychological and physical disturbances that the researchers felt provided a link to the various personalities manifested in the apparitions. The religious theme, for example, that ran throughout the haunting "could be related to feelings of conflict engendered by Mrs. Berini's conversion to Catholicism [from Judaism]," said Roll and Tringale.

But, they concluded, "these interpretations are, of course, speculative, and must wait on future research before we can take them seriously. Though it seemed that Mrs. Berini played an important role in providing or directing the energy that animated the contents of her home, the incidents cannot be understood in terms of her personality alone." And so another haunting episode came to a close as mysteriously as it began, leaving investigators no closer to an understanding of those phantom presences that have bedeviled so many households for so many centuries.

Haunted Washington

By day, the landmarks and monuments of Washington, D.C., seem to be proud and elegant symbols of politics and power, worthy affirmations of designer Pierre L'Enfant's ambition to create a capital city "magnificent enough to grace a great nation."

At night, however, as shadows fall across the white facades and marble columns, a very different Washington can emerge. From the graceful dome of the Capitol, to the White House, to the mansions of Georgetown and Embassy Row, familiar buildings lose their stately luster to an ominous darkening, taking on the aspect of shadowy mausoleums. It is at these times, some say, that ghosts walk the corridors of power, reliving old disputes and remembering sorrows long forgotten by the living.

For nearly 200 years, the District of Columbia has been alive with stories of restless spirits and vengeful phantoms. Some of these supernatural tales involve the famous and powerful, while others concern the downtrodden and forgotten; all of them are part of the strange and haunting mystery that envelops the capital.

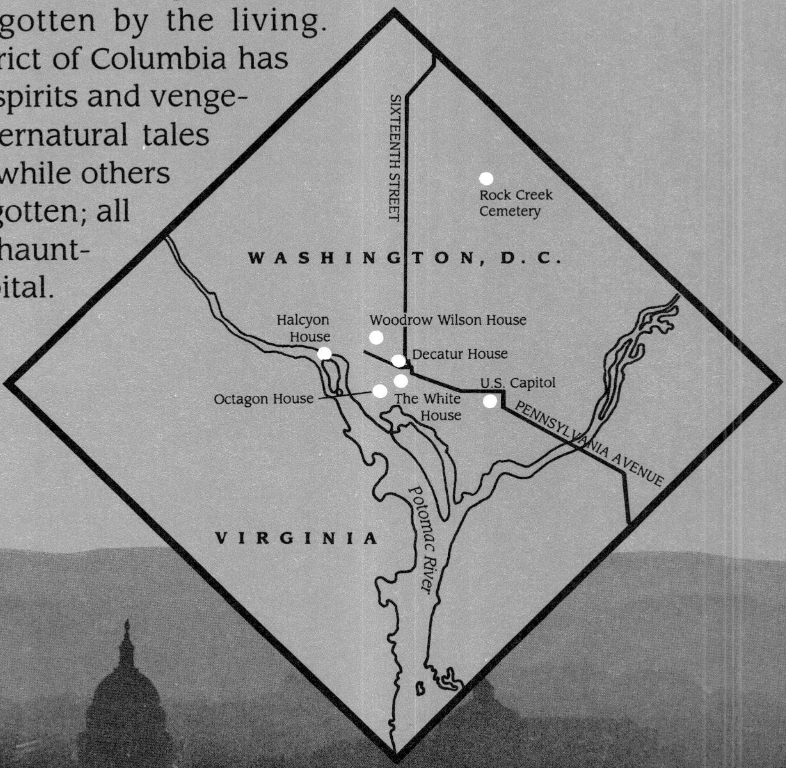

SIXTEENTH STREET

Rock Creek Cemetery

W A S H I N G T O N, D. C.

Halcyon House

Woodrow Wilson House

Decatur House

Octagon House

The White House

U.S. Capitol

PENNSYLVANIA AVENUE

Potomac River

V I R G I N I A

Ghosts beneath the Capitol Dome

Almost from the moment George Washington laid its cornerstone in 1793, the United States Capitol has been rife with phantoms. Perhaps the first was that of a stonemason who, during the Capitol's construction, had the misfortune to be plastered into a hardening wall. Legend holds that the man lost an argument with a brick-wielding carpenter, who then used the mason's own trowel to seal his tomb.

Other ghostly residents of the Capitol are purported to include Presidents John Quincy Adams and James Garfield, the Unknown Soldier of World War I, and a huge demon cat that prowls the narrow marble halls by night. Even the stone figures of those memorialized in Statuary Hall have reportedly come down off their pedestals each New Year's Eve to celebrate the health of the United States of America.

Two former Speakers of the House of Representatives, Joseph G. Cannon and Champ Clark, are possibly the most frequent spirit visitors to the Capitol. Bitter political foes, the two men faced off in the House chamber when Clark, the progressive Democratic floor leader, led his party in a heated revolt against the more conservative Cannon.

Although the two men eventually settled their differences in life, some believe the debate continues to rage in the world beyond. Capitol guards have reported hearing the rap of a gavel on the Speaker's dais in the dead of night and, upon peering into the House chamber to investigate, seeing the contentious Clark and Cannon squaring off once more *(left)*.

Dark stains on the marble steps of the House gallery *(above)* mark the site of a Washington murder—and the Capitol's most chilling mystery. The strange story began in the winter of 1890, when Kentucky congressman William Taulbee and Charles Kincaid, a newspaperman, angrily confronted each other in the hallway outside the House press gallery. Taulbee, furious over a disparaging article the journalist had printed in his newspaper, demanded an apology and retraction. No apology was forthcoming. Instead, the hot-headed Kincaid pulled out a pistol and shot the congressman dead.

To this day, the ugly, pale red splotches said to be Taulbee's lifeblood are visible on the steps where he fell. Maintenance staff have tried repeatedly, over the years, to erase the stains—but to no avail. Capitol workers swear they have seen and heard the congressman's spirit lingering at the spot, and even now, whenever a journalist happens to stumble on the slick marble stairway, Taulbee's spirit is thought to be taking its revenge.

Restless Presidents

Even the White House has its phantoms. The supposed spirit of President Abraham Lincoln is sometimes sighted roaming the halls, and Thomas Jefferson has reportedly been heard practicing his violin in the Yellow Oval Room. For nearly 150 years, the sound of deep, throaty laughter has been heard from the elegant Queen's Bedroom *(below)*. Among its furnishings is a canopied four-poster bed said to have belonged to Andrew Jackson, and some believe the mysterious laughter could only be his.

President Jackson had something of a reputation as a rakish character. His attentions toward the beautiful wife of one of his cabinet officers sparked a scandal that finally led to the man's resignation.

Apparently, the scandal continued to trouble Jackson in the afterworld. Within twenty years of the president's death in 1845, Mary Todd Lincoln claimed to have heard his spirit swearing and stomping about in the room, although the ribald laughter reported by others suggests that Jackson ultimately found some solace.

More recently, Mrs. Lillian Rogers Parks, who spent thirty years on the White House staff, related an encounter of a different sort. While hemming a bedspread in the Queen's Bedroom during the Eisenhower administration, Mrs. Parks felt a presence close by. "I could feel something coldish behind me," she recalled, "and I didn't have the courage to look. It's hard to explain. I went out of the room, and I didn't finish that spread until three years later."

In 1921, after two terms as president, an ailing Woodrow Wilson moved to a mansion off Washington's Embassy Row. He spent his time quietly, moving slowly with the aid of a cane, studying his books and papers, and often brooding over his unsuccessful fight to gain congressional approval for U.S. participation in the League of Nations. Close associates reported that the former president was troubled by lapses of memory and "unpredictable crying spells."

Wilson died after only three years in the house, but some believe that his spirit lingers on. A caretaker at the Wilson House, now a museum, once reported that he heard the slow shuffle of a man with a cane climbing the stairs; others have heard the muffled sounds of a man's sobs.

Wilson's ghost is known to have been sighted only once. A cleaning woman, entering the bedroom one day, caught sight of a bespectacled figure sitting in the president's favorite rocking chair *(right)*. Startled, she blinked and looked again. The figure had vanished, but the empty chair continued to rock back and forth.

A Naval Hero and Runaway Slaves

On a March night in 1820, Stephen Decatur, America's foremost naval hero, stood in somber reflection at the window of his home on Washington's Lafayette Square. With four wars behind him, Decatur had thought his fighting days were over. The next day, however, he was obliged to fight an unwanted duel with a naval officer he had helped to court-martial years before; the man blamed him for a failed career and pursued the quarrel to this grim solution.

Just before dawn, Decatur slipped out of the back door of his home, carrying his dueling pistol in a black box beneath his arm. Hours later, friends bore him home with a fatal wound. As he lay dying, Decatur anguished over the futility of his unhappy end. "If it were in the cause of my country," he said, "it would be nothing."

Within a year, Decatur's melancholy spirit was reported at the window where he had stood the night before his death *(left)*. The window was ordered walled up, but passersby continued to catch sight of a transparent figure standing at the spot, gazing despondently over the estate. Apparently, the captain's fate continues to torment him. Other witnesses have seen a figure slipping through the house's back entrance, just as Decatur did on the morning of his death. Beneath its arm, they say, the figure carries a small black box.

In the garden and basement of Georgetown's Halcyon House *(above)*, built in 1787 for its splendid view of the Potomac River, unearthly whispers and low moans have served as eerie reminders of the mansion's later use as a link in the so-called underground railroad, which aided runaway slaves in their flights to freedom. A secret tunnel led from the edge of the Potomac into the house's cellar, but many of the escaped slaves, weakened by their arduous flight, made the river crossing only to die in the underground chamber. Their final cries, it is said, echo to this day.

A carpenter, hired in the early 1900s to seal up the tunnel, heard the moans and sobs as he worked. Although he tried to dismiss them as a trick of wind, the sounds unnerved him and haunted him for the rest of his life. "It's been 50 to 60 years," he recalled shortly before his death. "Guess I'll carry those ghostly cries to my grave."

Private Griefs, Public Hauntings

Built in 1800 by Colonel John Tayloe, the magnificent Octagon House was the scene of a romantic tragedy. A few years after Tayloe moved his family into the house, one of his daughters fell in love with a British officer, much to the colonel's displeasure. Despite his daughter's entreaties, Tayloe even refused to allow the Englishman in his home. One night, after a bitter argument had failed to change her father's mind, the distraught girl grabbed a candle and ran up the stairs toward her room. A moment later, the family heard a shrill cry, followed by a horrifying thud. Racing toward the sound, Tayloe found his daughter's lifeless body crumpled at the foot of the winding staircase.

Ever since then, the three-story stairway of Octagon House has been believed to be haunted. Flickering shadows, like those cast by a candle, have been seen slowly ascending the steps, followed moments later by a woman's shriek and the sound of a sickening impact. At the spot where the girl fell, nothing is seen or felt but a shadowy stillness, grown strangely cold.

In a holly-shaded grove of the Rock Creek Cemetery, Washington's oldest burial ground, sits one of the most curious of the city's many statues. More than six feet in height, the bronze figure is neither male nor female and is unmarked by inscription or date. A cloak and cowl throw the impassive face into eternal shadow, shielding downturned eyes.

The disquieting statue is an oddly fitting memorial to Marian Adams, whose death more than a century ago fueled a Washington scandal. The wife of Henry Adams, the noted historian and descendant of Presidents John Adams and John Quincy Adams, Marian was a quiet woman of sharp intelligence and wide learning, possessed of what Henry James called "intellectual grace."

On a December night in 1885, Adams came home to find his wife unconscious before the fire. A physician was summoned, but he arrived too late to save her. Immediately, rumors began to circulate. Although Mrs. Adams had been in poor health, her death came as a surprise and was widely thought to have been a suicide.

Henry Adams remained silent about the circumstances of his wife's death, but the statue he ordered to mark her grave only excited more speculation. Many were struck by the odd fact that the figure in no way resembled the late Mrs. Adams. Indeed, Adams had instructed the sculptor, the famed Augustus Saint-Gaudens, that "no . . . attempt is to be made to make it intelligible to the average mind."

Intelligible or not, the statue produces an overpowering feeling of sorrow and coldness in all who see it. Although the sculptor called his work *The Mystery of the Hereafter*, it is more commonly known simply as *Grief*. Some who have sat before the hooded figure report that the despairing eyes actually appeared to come to life, while others, seated alone at dusk, claim to have been joined by the frail and sad-eyed figure of a woman clothed in the style of the late nineteenth century.

112

CHAPTER 4

Haunters and Hunters

he eerie events at Ash Manor reportedly began in the early summer of 1934, shortly after a man by the name of Maurice Kelly bought the thirteenth-century house and its attendant twenty-four forested acres in Sussex, England. Hardly had Kelly moved in with his wife, Katherine, and their fourteen-year-old daughter than the family was disturbed by noises coming from the attic. It sounded as if someone were stamping on the floorboards—which was impossible, since the flooring had long since been removed, leaving only the bare joists.

The noises were unsettling, but by no means unnerving enough to compel the new owner to decamp. Kelly was a no-nonsense businessman who had acquired the estate for a song and was well pleased with his bargain. He was not disposed to flee phenomena that could reasonably be written off as sounds to which many old houses are naturally prone. But on the night of November 18, his comfortable rationale began to slip.

Kelly was startled out of a deep sleep by three loud thumps on his bedroom door. Arising, he walked down the hallway to his wife's quarters. Had she heard anything? "Yes," she replied, "three violent bangs." As Kelly would eventually tell an investigator of the paranormal, at exactly the same time—3:45 a.m.—on the next night, he was wakened by two knocks on the door, and on the following night by one. For several ensuing nights, while Kelly was away on a business trip, silence prevailed at Ash Manor. Yet horror was close at hand. Retiring on the evening of his return, he felt strangely uneasy. "The room was unnaturally cold," he said later, "and there was something unpleasant about it." Kelly drifted off into sleep about 3:00 a.m.—only to have his slumber shattered by a crashing knock on the door.

"I sat up with a jerk," he recalled. "Standing in the doorway I saw a little oldish man, dressed in a green smock, very muddy breeches and gaiters, a slouch hat on his head and a handkerchief around his neck." To Kelly, there was nothing ghostly about the intruder, who appeared to be solidly human. Supposing that a tramp had somehow gotten into the house, Kelly shouted: "Who are you? What do you want in my house?" Receiving no reply, Kelly leaped from his bed and tried to seize the visitor's shoulder. The last thing he remembered was that his hand passed right through the figure.

As Mrs. Kelly recalled the event, she had heard "an appalling scream," and then her husband ran into her room and fainted. "His face was livid, his eyes were bulging, and terror was written over every line of his countenance," she said. Afraid he was dying, her first thought was to fetch some medicinal brandy, and she rushed down the corridor to a room where the key to the wine cellar was kept. Returning to her husband, she saw in his bedroom doorway a small man. Although Kelly had fainted before he could tell her what he himself had seen, her description of the stranger tallied with her husband's in every detail—and she added a few of her own.

"His face was very red," she said, "the eyes malevolent and horrid, the mouth open and dribbling." Daunting as the stranger was, Katherine Kelly faced up to him. "What do you want?" she demanded. "Who are you?" Answered by silence, she swung a fist at the trespasser, only to have it pass through him and slam into the door lintel.

During the following months, according to the Kellys, the phantom night sounds continued. Worse yet, they saw "the green man," as they came to call him, as many as two dozen times. Once, Mrs. Kelly recalled, the apparition deliberately raised its head to display a gaping wound "all around his neck. Something horrible was sticking out, like a cut windpipe."

The beleaguered Kellys sought help from a priest, who invoked God's blessing on the house. The attempted exorcism only made matters worse. "For two nights," said Mrs. Kelly, "I knelt outside my door, praying and fighting some tangible force of evil." In desperation, Kelly placed a magazine advertisement asking for expert help. It was answered by two alleged ghost hunters who spun an inventive tale about the ghost of a nineteenth-century cobbler seeking revenge on a milkmaid who had spurned his advances. After assuring the Kellys that they would no longer be bothered, the pair collected a tidy fee and left. But the haunting of Ash Manor continued.

Finally, in July 1936, the Kellys' plight came to the attention of Dr. Nandor Fodor, a psychoanalyst with an avid interest in the paranormal. At the time he took up the Kellys' troubles, Fodor had recently been named chief researcher for the London-based International Institute for Psychical Research. Arriving at Ash Manor, he set about his work in orderly fashion. First, he inspected the premises, assuring himself that the mysterious noises could not be explained by structural defects. Then he interviewed Kelly, who struck him as "a hardheaded, stubborn materialist in no way inclined toward psychic matters." Next, Fodor took an affidavit from Mrs. Kelly and interviewed the daughter, Patricia. As a final preparatory step, Fodor rigged a camera on Ash Manor's stairway landing, where the apparition had, according to the Kellys, frequently been seen.

Photographing ghosts was, and remains, an enterprise of questionable effectiveness, but Fodor was clearly satisfied that it could be done. "By the use of a quartz lens and specially sensitized plates," he said, "the receptivity from the invisible parts of the spectrum can be increased. Thus, a ghost, though invisible to us, might be photographed, provided it appeared in focus within the right range of ultraviolet radiation."

His gear in place, the doctor began what he would later call his "ghostly vigil." At one time during the night he was startled by two loud thumps from the direction of Patricia's room, but they were not of spectral origin. It turned out that the girl, annoyed at being confined in her room to keep her out of the way of the investigation, had stamped on the floor. Later, Fodor heard an ominous gurgling sound—only to find that Mrs. Kelly was gargling mouthwash before going to bed. "I did not fall asleep until 6:15 in the morning," Fodor recalled. "During the night, I exposed several plates. None of them showed anything."

A second night-long vigil also failed to produce results, but Fodor persevered. As it happened, the famous American medium Eileen Garrett was in England at the time, and she responded to Fodor's call for assistance. On the night of July 25, 1936, seated in front of a yawning fireplace in the gloomy old house, Garrett went into a trance and, it seemed, was soon possessed by a discarnate entity named Uvani, supposedly a long-dead Arab who oversaw the access of other spirits to the medium during most of her séances. How, asked Fodor, could the haunting of Ash Manor be explained? At that, Uvani allowed that he would stand aside and permit the invading ghost to take over Garrett's body and speak for himself.

The medium's breathing grew heavy, her body stiff, and by Fodor's account, her features became those "of a tortured man, cheeks sunken in, mouth half open, and an expression of untold agony over the countenance." Garrett beckoned to Fodor to approach, then reached out and seized his hand in a grip so powerful that he shouted in pain. In a strangled voice, the medium cried, *"Eleison! Eleison!"*—Greek for "mercy, mercy." Speaking in broken, often incomprehensible phrases, apparently couched in archaic English, the presumed spirit begged to be reunited with his wife. "Prythee, friend," he said through the medium, "find me her resting place. Thou art friend. Find for me my wife." The apparition, if such he was, raged against "Buckingham"—presumably one of the English dukes of

Ash Manor in Sussex, England, was said to harbor the ghost of a sixteenth-century man seeking vengeance against the seducer of his wife. The specter was supposedly exorcised in 1936 by medium Eileen Garrett.

This ghostly image appeared in a photograph made by an Ash Manor grounds-keeper, who trained his camera on the corner of a stair landing that the apparition was said to frequent. The servant disputed a critic's suggestion that the "ghost" was more likely a thumbprint on the negative.

that name. "He offered me ducats and broad acres for my wife," he said. "He my enemy. Leave me to rot here without my son. I wait for news from my son. He did this to me, this royal bastard. . . . May his soul burn forever in that hell from which there can be no escape."

Fodor summoned Maurice Kelly to the front of the room. Staring at Garrett, Kelly staggered and muttered, "It is the exact image of the ghost." Then Katherine Kelly came forward and, as Fodor later recounted, she "went the color of chalk." Covering her face with her hands, she sobbed "my God" and shrank away from the medium. Moments later, the spirit seemed to speak again, asking for a quill. Fodor handed over a pencil and notebook, and Garrett began writing in a peculiar script that some researchers later attested could not have been her own. "Henley," she scrawled. Then: "Edward Charles." And finally: "Esse," which, as it turned out, had once been the name of a village near Ash Manor.

The ghost's name in life apparently had been Henley, and the gist of his story was this: He and Buckingham had been childhood friends, but as adults they had a falling out over Buckingham's lust for Henley's wife, Dorothy. "He forced her eyes," ranted the ghost. The precise meaning of the phrase was unclear, but its import seemed to be that Buckingham had seduced Dorothy, so outraging Henley that his ghost still clung to earth, thirsting for redress. "Do not leave me," the spirit pleaded with Fodor, "but help me to attain my vengeance." Vengeance, Fodor replied, should be left to God. "You prate to me of God," cried the ghost. "He let me suffer. I want my vengeance."

Fodor was well acquainted with the notion shared by many occultists that hatred and revenge were among the most common motives keeping spirits earthbound. The ghosts could only find release, the theory went, by relinquishing these passions. With that in mind, the investigator tried persuasion. "You can be free and happy if you give up your thoughts of vengeance which tie you to earth," he said. "Which do you want: your vengeance or to join your wife and son?" The spirit hesitated, sought to evade the question, and finally decided: "For them, yes."

"At that moment," wrote Fodor, "something seemed to happen to him. He cried out and grasped my hand again: 'Hold me, hold me! I cannot stay. I am slipping. Don't leave me, don't leave me!' " And the body of Eileen Garrett slumped back into her chair. The ghost of Ash Manor appeared to be gone.

But not for long. The very next evening, a distraught Kelly called Fodor. "He's here again!" Kelly exclaimed. "He's standing in the doorway, opening his mouth and trying to speak." Fodor went to Garrett's London flat to discuss the ghost's reappearance. Again the medium appeared to enter a trance, whereupon her spirit guide declared his thoughts on the specter's persistence. Henley's spirit was nourished, Uvani said, by tensions within the Kelly family itself. Not until the strains were eased would the specter take its final leave.

Confronted by this pronouncement, the distraught Kellys told an unhappy story: Kelly was a homosexual, and to alleviate her sexual frustrations, his wife had become a morphine addict. Fodor later wrote that the Kellys had used the ghost as "a distracting element, a sort of tranquilizer, which helped to hold the family together." He hastened to add that the apparition was no less real for all that. In any case, the confession seemed to bring relief. Whatever his origins and nature, and whatever emotional fodder fueled him—his own sad passions or those of others—the Ash Manor ghost was seen no more.

There are skeptics who would dismiss the Ash Manor case out of hand, if for no other reason than Nandor Fodor was the chief teller of the tale, and he was not the most credible of ghost hunters. He seemed to have a yen to believe in the ghosts he sought, so his objectivity was in question. Nonetheless, his ghost-hunting avocation put him in the company of a special and widely misunderstood breed. It has seldom been the primary mission of these psychical investigators to "lay the ghost," as dispelling a spirit is called in their parlance. Rather, ridding dwellings of haunting specters—if that should happen—is only a by-product of their quest to determine the reality of a spectral world and, assuming it is real, to study its nature. For as long as ghosts have haunted human consciousness, humans have, in a sense, haunted ghosts, trying relentlessly to discover whether they are actual revenants from beyond the grave or merely the effluvia of distorted perceptions and passions of the living.

In the quest for answers, ghost hunters have evolved a variety of techniques. Sometimes a particular method has come into vogue and then been discarded, only to be revived in light of further experience. Mediums, for example, were for many years considered to be the best channels for communicating with spirits of the dead. Around the middle of the twentieth century, however, the study of psychic phenomena, which has always been tightly entwined with the study of ghosts, largely moved from séance rooms to laboratories and classrooms under the influence of psychical researcher Joseph Banks Rhine of Duke University. He relied on scientific method, not spiritualism, and his experiments produced what some parapsychologists believed to be significant evidence of extrasensory perception. But the question of whether such talents as telepathy and clairvoyance—even if they did exist—figured in communicating with the dead was never the prime focus of Rhine and his colleagues, and it remained unanswered. In recent years, critics have found flaws in Rhine's methodology, and some investigators have returned to time-honored standbys. Mediums are again widely used, although the modern tendency is to approach them armed with whatever sensitive instruments of detection modern technology can provide.

No matter what system the investigator uses, his search is apt to be beset by difficulties. Hauntings often go on for prolonged periods, and the hunter sometimes waits for weeks or even months for a purported ghost to manifest itself. Meanwhile, the lives of those who dwell in houses they think are haunted can be seriously disturbed by the presence of the hunter and his or her equipment. Sometimes, in fact, such families come to believe that the ghost is less bother than the human probing its essence. Moreover, specters rarely cooperate with their hunters. Some investigators believe that the mere presence of one of their number can cause a ghost to remain quiescent for months.

Even on those infrequent occasions when a psychical investigator does believe himself to be in contact with a haunting spirit, he must beware of accepting what it says at face value—if only because, as the author and journalist G. K. Chesterton once wrote, ghosts lie. So, alas, do humans, and in undertaking an investigation it is essential for the ghost hunter to determine whether an alleged haunting might not be best explained in terms of mendacity, fraud, hysteria, or the workings of mundane nature.

According to Andrew MacKenzie, a leading authority on hauntings, "A normal explanation for an experience

An Eccentric's War on Ghosts

Among the countless oddities in the Winchester House are, clockwise from the top, a staircase that dead-ends at a ceiling; a short door for short ghosts; a switchback stairway, with seven turns and forty-four steps, rising only nine feet; and a door that opens onto a skylight frame poised above a two-story drop.

An aerial view of the Winchester House shows the results of thirty-eight years of nonstop building.

In 1862, a tiny young woman named Sarah Pardee married William Wirt Winchester. In time, she would come to believe that she had also married his curse. Winchester was the son of the inventor and manufacturer of Winchester rifles. After the younger Winchester died in 1881, Sarah was told by a Boston medium that his death had been caused by spirits of the untold thousands killed by Winchester rifles. Sarah stood to inherit the hauntings along with the Winchester millions, the medium said. Her only escape was to buy a house and constantly expand it. The reasoning seemed to be that she might thereby attract a better class of ghosts to protect her from the grubby and vindictive sort.

Sarah Winchester moved to California in 1884 and bought an 8-room farmhouse in San Jose. Six months later, the house had 26 rooms, and still construction continued around the clock. So it went for the next thirty-eight years until the reclusive widow died in 1922 at the age of eighty-five. By then, the house had 160 rooms and sprawled over six acres. Its manifold architectural oddities were supposedly dictated by the aristocratic spirits whom Sarah cultivated. Most of the peculiarities seemed designed either to accommodate the classy ghosts or to confuse the spectral rabble.

must first be sought before we accept a paranormal one." A devoted advocate of that doctrine, British researcher G. W. Lambert in 1960 issued the results of an extensive study of the correlation between London's supposedly haunted buildings and their proximity to tidal streams that had been "built over or otherwise hidden from sight."

Of the twenty-five cases listed by Lambert in the *Journal of the Society for Psychical Research,* no fewer than twenty were either atop or near subterranean waterways. Moreover, Lambert discovered a significant relationship between reported hauntings and periods when the rainfall in London had been abnormally heavy. Lambert's theory: Immense hydraulic pressures built up underground by excessive rainfall may, in effect, jack up a building, thereby causing it to tilt. When the pressure eventually eases, the structure suddenly subsides, creating the loud noises and even the moving objects that are frequently associated with hauntings and with poltergeists.

A year earlier, Lambert had reported on a study of fifty Scottish sites where paranormal happenings had been reported. Nineteen were in the limestone region around the Firth of Forth, where underground streams abound. Of the rest, all but three were near geological faults, where quakes and shakes of the earth are common. Lambert discovered that most of the ghostly events had occurred during periods of high seismic activity. "The contention here," he wrote, "is that a jolt imparted to a house from underground . . . can be transmitted through the structure of the building to loose objects in the rooms, sending them 'flying,' and that this can happen without any damage to the house, if it is on a firm foundation." Needless to add, earth tremors also produce weird noises. Therein may lie at least a partial solution to one of psychic history's most baffling mysteries—the hauntings at Ballechin House.

Early on the evening of February 3, 1897, Ada Goodrich Freer, an ethereally beautiful woman, and her companion, Constance Moore, a daughter of Queen Victoria's chaplain, trudged through deep snow to the doorway of Ballechin House in the remote Scottish Highlands overlooking the shadowed valley of the Tay. Even before she entered the place, Freer was filled with a sense of dread. "The house looked very gloomy," she wrote later, and once inside, "It felt like a vault." For Freer, who had been sent to the scene as an

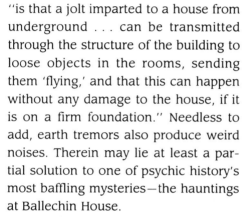

In a 1965 photograph taken near the Tower of London, British psychical researcher G. W. Lambert (right) and a colleague, John Cutten, stand before a Cutten invention called a vibrograph. The device was supposed to detect minute movements in the air or ground. Lambert believed many "ghostly" manifestations resulted simply from buildings shifting in response to subsurface hydraulic pressures.

investigator for the Society for Psychical Research, Ballechin House was rich in the sort of history to which she was strongly attracted.

Built in 1806 on the hereditary estate of the Steuart family, descendents of Scotland's King Robert II, Ballechin House by 1850 had come into the possession of Major Robert Steuart, a retired officer of the East India Company. By any standard, Steuart was a peculiar fellow. A bachelor and a misanthrope, he populated the house with fourteen dogs, including a large black spaniel that was his favorite. During his years in India, the major had come to believe in the transmigration of souls, and he was fond of declaring that after his death he would return to earth in the body of the black spaniel.

For human companionship, Steuart had only his housekeeper, a young woman named Sarah, who died in 1873 under circumstances locally described as mysterious. Neighborhood tongues wagged when it was learned that she had passed away in Steuart's bedroom, and they wagged even more when, after his own death in 1876, his will decreed that he be buried next to Sarah.

To Robert Steuart's heirs, the promised transmigration of their eccentric, disagreeable, and slightly disreputable relative was clearly an unwelcome eventuality; and in a move to prevent it, they shot all his dogs—starting with the spaniel. The heir to Ballechin House was John Steuart, a nephew and a devout Roman Catholic who soon converted a cottage on the estate into a retreat for nuns.

The hauntings began soon after John Steuart and his family moved in. Working one day on her household accounts, Mrs. Steuart was assailed by a pervasive odor of dogs, familiar to her from the days when canines filled the old major's house. And as she moved to open a window, she felt rubbing against her legs an invisible presence that she somehow knew to be that of a dog.

During the years that followed, residents of Ballechin House reported being constantly disturbed by nocturnal noises—inexplicable knocks; sharp, explosive sounds; even the angry voices of people who, although their words were indistinguishable, seemed to be quarreling. Especially alarming were the distinctive footsteps of someone—or something—limping around the room where Sarah had died. Major Robert Steuart had returned from India with a pronounced limp.

In the summer of 1892, a Jesuit priest named Father Hayden arrived at Ballechin House to tend to the spiritual needs of the nuns at the cottage. On eight of the nine nights that he slept in the manor, he said, he was disturbed by "very queer and extraordinary noises." From somewhere between his bed and the ceiling came sounds "like continuous explosion of petards." From time to time he heard what he thought was "a large animal" flinging itself against his door. Yet when he peered into the hallway, nothing was there. "Nothing," the priest wrote later, "could induce me to pass another night there . . . and in other respects I do not think I am a coward."

Three years later, while visiting in London, John Steuart was run over and killed by a hansom cab. With him dead, Ballechin House was taken over by another Steuart, an army captain who had no desire to live there. Instead, in 1896, he leased the property to a wealthy family who paid a year's rent in advance for the dubious privilege of staying in the house and shooting grouse on the extensive grounds. But after a mere seven weeks of occupancy fraught with fearsome nocturnal sounds, the new tenants fled without so much as stopping to seek a rebate for the unused part of the lease.

To John Crichton-Stuart, third marquis of Bute and an enthusiast of the paranormal, the unscheduled vacancy at Ballechin House was an opportunity he had long awaited. Having first heard its ghostly lore several years earlier from Father Hayden, Bute now decided to sponsor a full investigation. He got help for the project from the Society for Psychical Research, which assigned to the case two of its investigators—Colonel Lemesurier Taylor, a veteran researcher, and Ada Goodrich Freer. With Bute footing the bill, Taylor leased Ballechin House in his own name. However, family affairs prevented his traveling there at that time, and it was thus Freer and her companion who arrived at the house in advance of a large group of guests, chosen by Freer and Taylor partly because they were unaware of the manor's sinister background and partly because they were deemed either sensitive to, or open-minded about, ghostly occurrences.

As a rule, ghost hunters must resign themselves to waiting weeks or months before incumbent spirits are willing to perform. But not Ada Freer. According to the 250-page book that she subsequently wrote about the case, she was awakened on her very first night by "a loud clanging sound, which seemed to resound through the house." A little later, both Freer and her friend Constance Moore heard voices, and the next night they were perplexed by what sounded like a priest saying his office. (That, as it turned out, was one of the most common phenomena at Ballechin House.)

On the following evening, Ada Freer and her guests consulted a

John Crichton-Stuart, third marquis of Bute, leased Ballechin House (opposite page) for an 1897 probe of its reputed ghosts. Later, he co-wrote a book on the hauntings with one of the investigators, Ada Goodrich Freer.

Ouija board, whose planchette promptly spelled out a message from a spirit calling itself Ishbel, instructing the humans to go at dusk "to the glen in the avenue, up by the burn." (A burn is a stream.) Shortly after sundown the following day, Freer set out for the appointed place with two male companions. "It was quite dark," she wrote, "but the snow gleamed so white we could see our way. . . . I saw a slight black figure, a woman, moving slowly up the glen. She stopped, and turned and looked at me. She was dressed as a nun." One of old Major Robert Steuart's sisters, Isabella, had been a nun until her death in 1880.

Later, Freer said, she saw the ghostly nun many times. Sometimes the shade was in solemn conversation with the phantom of an older woman, who appeared to be scolding her. Once, Freer reported, the nun was weeping in a manner that "seemed to me to be passionate and unrestrained." Interestingly, however, neither of the men who accompanied Freer on the first visit to the stream was able to see the spectral nun. And although several Ballechin House guests

in the night. Finally, shortly before she ended her investigation, Freer was awakened one night by the terrified whimpering of her dog, a Pomeranian named Spooks. Sitting up, she "saw two black paws [not Spooks's] resting on the table beside the bed. It gave me a sickening sensation."

All in all, it would appear that Ballechin House and its grounds were haunted, either visibly or invisibly, by at least nine spirits: the nun Ishbel (or Isabella), Ishbel's older companion (perhaps Margaret, another sister of Major Robert Steuart's), the man with a limp (presumably Major Steuart), the shuffling man, the old woman with half a body, the woman with the crucifix, a dead priest, a living priest, and a black dog.

Ada Freer and her guests left Ballechin House in May 1897. Thereafter, as far as anyone knows, the place remained tranquil until it was finally razed in 1963. Its ghosts were apparently gone.

But had they, in fact, ever existed? Although it was recognized even at the time of Freer's investigation that sounds associated with spirits might be explained in terms of such natural causes as underground water or earth tremors, Lambert's research revived that possibility in the case of Ballechin House. The old building, he noted, was close to the spots where two streams go underground, and one of the wettest months in British history had occurred during the investigation. Moreover, the Steuart estate lay near the great fault line that runs southwest across Scotland from Stonehaven, a region in which 465 shocks had been recorded in one thirty-eight-year period.

If natural causes could be ascribed to the auditory phenomena at Ballechin House, the tactile and visual manifestations posed more perplexing problems. Still, Ada Freer was widely known to be highly susceptible to psychic experiences, real or imagined; her senses were excited even before she set foot in Ballechin House, and there is no reason

subsequently claimed to have seen various specters, including the nun, their testimony left even Freer unconvinced.

Still, there were phenomena enough at Ballechin House to satisfy the greediest ghost hunter. During the sixty-nine days and nights that Freer and her company stayed there, extraordinary noises were reported on ninety-two separate occasions. These included moans, groans, screams, knocks, clangs, thuds, and explosive bangs, along with the sounds of the limping man, the reading priest, moving animals, and the shuffling footsteps of someone presumed to be an elderly man. Four persons, including Freer and a housemaid, said they had been touched by invisible presences. The most common sensation was that of having one's bed lifted or rocked or of having something tug at one's bedclothing. Both Freer and Constance Moore said they had been pushed by a large, invisible dog, and a female guest claimed that she had actually wrestled with an unseen phantom presence.

Of all phenomena, however, visual sightings are the most exciting to a psychical investigator, and Ballechin House was home to a kaleidoscope of ghosts. In addition to the nun and her companion, Freer saw a woman holding a crucifix. A housemaid witnessed the nighttime appearance of the upper half of an old woman. There was also a report of the apparition of a person who was still living but far from the premises—Father Hayden, the priest who had, five years previously, been so alarmed by things that went bump

An Ancient Ritual Ousts a Phantom

By noting the markings on painted wooden plaques, Lama Yeshe Dorje Rinpoche divines the identity of a dangerous ghost—allegedly the reincarnation of a dead schoolteacher.

Chanting a litany of exorcism, the lama stabs an effigy into which he has sealed the vital essence of the ghost. With this act, the priest destroys the evil entity and releases the teacher's spirit to await a more propitious rebirth. The effigy is cut into pieces.

After the ritual killing of the ghost, the priest cremates the effigy's remains, along with some of the paraphernalia used in the exorcism. The ashes are collected for burial.

Eons before Buddhism came to the primal fastness of Tibet, natives there practiced an animistic religion called Bon, a shamanistic faith replete with elaborate rituals. Many of these rites were peacefully incorporated into Tibetan Buddhism and are still practiced today. One of them, called *shedür,* is for the exorcism of ghosts.

The pictures on these two pages show parts of the ritual as it was performed in 1981 in Dharamsala, India, where many Tibetans fled after the Chinese invaded their country in 1950.

Presiding over the ceremony was Lama Yeshe Dorje Rinpoche, a priest in service to the Dalai Lama, spiritual leader of the Tibetan Buddhists.

The six-day ritual was undertaken after omens showed that the spirit of a man who had taught at a school for Tibetan children had been reincarnated as a hungry ghost—a malign spirit that supposedly can harm the living.

The complex ritual always begins with the lama's invoking a fiercely protective goddess called a *dakini,* ritually transforming himself into her in order to take on her strength and cleverness. The metamorphosis usually takes an entire day. Then the priest-deity uses painted wooden plaques in a divination rite designed to pinpoint, amid a horde of the 84,000 ghosts believed to exist, the particular one being sought. The plaques are placed in an iron pot, and the ritual of sorting through them to identify the threatening spirit generally requires three days.

In the 1981 ceremony, once the hungry ghost was found, the core of the exorcism began—the task of killing the ghost and thus releasing the teacher's spirit to seek a happier rebirth. To this end, the lama used an effigy, modeled from barley flour and butter, to serve as a container for the ghost's life force. While chanting spells aimed at preventing the ghost's escape from the doll, the priest stabbed it with a ritual dagger, then carved it into several pieces. The remains were burned in the same pot used for the divination ceremony—burning that assured the ghost's destruction and the release of the teacher's spirit.

On the fourth day of the exorcism, the lama and his attendants carried the effigy's ashes to a communal cremation ground for burial, which was accompanied by prayers and chanting.

The final phase of the exhausting rite involved two days spent in constructing elaborate thread crosses—geometric forms made from multihued thread and designed to attract the attention of powerful gods. The crosses were displayed along with appropriate offerings to thank the potent spirits and to propitiate them, asking their forbearance for tolerating the disruptive exorcism rite on their territory.

The ashes are taken to a ghat, or cremation ground. In the foreground lies the iron cauldron that was used during the ghost's expulsion, along with a ladle employed to pour the butter that fed its ghost-rending fire.

The priest and his assistants chant over the ghost's sealed grave, which is crowned with a stone cairn, or stupa. The stupa marks the site as powerful and dangerous ground.

to suppose that she calmed down once she was within its walls. Indeed, even Freer's fellow investigator, Lemesurier Taylor, shrugged off her ghostly nun as being singularly lacking in "evidential value."

The amateur ghost hunters who were Freer's guests not only anticipated finding proof of spectral existence, but some seemed to be hoping for it. One guest, for example, told of sitting "late by my fire expecting, but as nothing seemed to be going to happen I went to bed, and soon to sleep." She was shortly awakened by what she took to be a shaking of her bed. However, she "refrained from striking a light, in order to see the next development of this weird experience. To my disappointment nothing happened." In short, as one visitor phrased it, at least some of the occupants of Ballechin House were "agape for wonders." It is surely possible that what they wanted to see, they saw—or thought they saw.

If human susceptibility to the power of suggestion helped spawn the ghosts at Ballechin House, then questions arise as to its role in other reports of ghostly phenomena—reports that are by no means uncommon. A 1984 survey by the University of Chicago's National Opinion Research Center showed that 42 percent of all Americans say that they have been in touch with someone who died, while a 1987 Epcot Center poll found that 13 percent claimed to have sighted a ghost.

In 1964, a chance to explore the potency of suggestion was inadvertently provided by a half-hour British television program called "The Unknown." To make their film, producers asked A. D. Cornell, a member of the SPR, to demonstrate how a skilled psychical investigator goes about his business. The film site was Morley Hall, a sixteenth-century mansion in Norfolk. Although the place had no reputation for being haunted, its dark and gloomy interior seemed a likely haven for unearthly things.

All one night Cornell went through his standard paces, interviewing the building's owner, inspecting the premises, setting up his detection instruments—and, as always, waiting in the dark for a spirit to appear. Next morning he stepped outside to be interviewed by the program's commentator. Had he found anything unusual? No, replied Cornell. Did he believe Morley Hall was haunted? No, he certainly did not.

After the program aired, however, five viewers wrote in to say that they had seen the ghostly figure of a monk standing to Cornell's right during the interview. Astonished, members of the television company's staff examined the film closely and saw nothing untoward. As an experiment, the interview was aired twice more. Without going into other details, an announcer simply said that some people had "reported seeing a ghost on the film."

Now, prompted by the suggestion that a phantom might be present, twenty-seven viewers replied. Fifteen said they had seen a monk or a priest. Ten others were more or less compatible with that notion; one described a lady in a mantilla and one a hooded skull. However, seven of the viewers were skeptical enough to attribute the spectral shape on the film to a trick of lighting or some other optical illusion—and they were right. At the time of the interview, Cornell had been standing in front of a large mullioned window. On looking closely at blow-ups of the film's frames, the program's producers finally found an image, vaguely resembling the form of a monk, that had been caused by discoloration in the window's stonework.

Nonetheless, most of the television viewers who responded were convinced that they had actually seen something supernatural. Considering the ruinous effect that such impressionable persons can have on serious psychic research, Cornell was moved to comment: "One is driven to wonder (although not very hopefully) whether it might not be possible to devise some way of 'screening' out any witnesses of an apparition who are liable to suffer from such extreme illusions."

But Cornell also believed that the idea of suggestibility as an explanation for ghosts could be carried too far. Most people, he argued, are not all that gullible. To prove his thesis, he conducted a series of tests. In one of them, beginning at 10:00 p.m. on May 26, 1960, Cornell draped himself in twelve feet of white sheeting. For seven minutes, while assistants hid in bushes to comfort any passersby who might be alarmed at the sight of a ghost, Cornell leaned against a tree in the churchyard of Saint Peter's church in Cambridge, adjacent to a cemetery and only eight feet from the university town's main thoroughfare. For the next five minutes he meandered about, sometimes in shadows, sometimes in the full glare of streetlights. Then he loitered around the tree for three more minutes before concluding the experiment with a five-minute stroll, during which he augmented his act with ghostly moaning.

During the twenty-minute performance, Cornell's "ghost" was within plain view of ninety passing vehicles, forty cyclists, and twelve pedestrians—but only two took more than passing notice of the ersatz apparition. One witness— a young man— stopped, stared, asked the spirit what it thought it was up to, and receiving no reply, began walking abreast of it. At that point, Cornell's assistants came out of hiding, explained the nature of the experiment, and asked what the fellow thought he had seen. His reply: "An art student walking around in a blanket." A few minutes later, an undergraduate cyclist got off his bike and stood gazing at the sheet-draped investigator. He too was asked what he believed the figure to be. The answer: "A man dressed up as a woman who surely must be mad."

Despite their interest in the possible effects of suggestion, psychical researchers are careful to make a distinction between suggestibility and sensitivity. For them, sensitivity is a talent owned by genuine mediums—people who seem to have special access to worlds invisible and inaudible to other humans. Such a person, apparently, was a woman known in psychic annals as the Seeress of Prevorst, after the Swabian village of her birth. Her real name was Friederike Hauffe, and

The delicate sensibilities of Ada Goodrich Freer are reflected in this 1894 photograph, taken three years before her investigation with the Society for Psychical Research of Ballechin House. Freer reported a spate of eerie events in her sixty-nine-day sojourn at the house, but critics doubted her, contending that Freer was impressionable and highly imaginative.

her case was recorded by Dr. Justinus A. C. Kerner, who in 1826 was called upon to treat her for a mysterious malady that had placed her on death's threshold. Kerner found a toothless, wasted, haggish woman who, since childhood, had supposedly fallen into mediumistic trances, experienced visions, and chatted with spirits of the dead. At the time Kerner met her, Hauffe was, among other things, closely associated with a poltergeist that rattled chains, threw gravel, hurled stools and lampshades about, and tugged off the sick woman's boots as she lay in bed.

Dubious at first, Kerner was soon convinced that the seeress had incredible powers. By his account, she could draw meticulous geometric figures, including perfect circles, at high speed in the dark. Even more amazing, she could lie on her bed with her eyes closed and easily read documents that Kerner placed on her bare stomach.

Moreover, Kerner contended, Hauffe sometimes used her special talents to root out ghosts. After hearing that a certain dwelling was haunted by the spirit of an old man, the investigator brought one of the house's residents to the seeress. She fell into a deep trance, during which she explained that a one-time burgomaster named Bellon had become an "earth-bound spirit" because he had, during his life, defrauded two orphans. Checking the records, Kerner found that in 1700 a Bellon had in fact been burgomaster—and director of an orphanage as well. Confronted by Hauffe's "evidence," Kerner related, the ghost admitted its guilt and vanished.

In dealing with Hauffe's life-threatening ailment, Kerner's treatment of choice was mesmerism, the once-voguish practice of stroking a body with magnets in an effort to stimulate the flow of certain theoretical "vital fluids" essential to good health. At first Hauffe seemed to respond favorably. Then, however, she grew progressively weaker. Kerner theorized that her strength was being drained by the spirits surrounding her. In 1829, Friederike Hauffe died. She was only twenty-eight years old.

Two decades later, the golden age of Spiritualism—the movement whose hallmark was mediums purporting to communicate with the dead—began when two adolescent sisters in upstate New York attracted enormous public attention by their apparent ability to talk with spirits. The sisters, Kate and Maggie Fox, were eventually debunked; nevertheless, the Spiritualist wave lasted until well into the twentieth century, when a flood of quacks and charlatans brought the movement into general disrepute. One of the few mediums to emerge with her reputation largely intact was Eileen Garrett, who helped rescue mediumship from its bog of chicanery and hocus-pocus and guide it toward its modern-day link with parapsychology.

According to her autobiography, the Irish-born Garrett experienced telepathic and clairvoyant episodes from childhood. She was host to a plethora of ostensible spirit guides, but unlike most mediums, she made no special claims about their origins or authenticity. She theorized, in fact, that her other-world contacts might well be no more than submerged fragments of her own personality. Garrett was even a little wary of her apparent psychic talents, concluding that they were "dangerous unless they are used to help people." Perhaps because of her doubts, she was indefatigable in searching for answers to explain the mediumistic experience. She made herself available for study by a number of parapsychologists, and in 1951, she founded the Parapsychology Foundation, based in New York, to fund scientific and scholarly research into the unknown. "If the whole strange, mystifying psychic gift could be snatched out of the darkness of séance rooms and put into the capable probing hands of science," she said, "everybody would feel much better about the subject." When Garrett died in 1970 at the age of seventy-seven, she was almost unanimously mourned and praised by her fellow researchers, even those who doubted—as she often doubted herself—that she had actually been in touch with spirits of the dead.

During her long career, Garrett was sometimes discouraged about her work. "All our investigations have been inconclusive," she once said. "I've taken part in so many experiments and have worked with so many investigators, I

The Emperor's Ghost

Rome is a city steeped in legend. One of the eeriest tales concerns Christian efforts to dispel the ghost of a pagan ruler whose many crimes included matricide and wife murder.

Legend has it that the emperor Nero, best remembered by history as a tyrant who persecuted Christians and allegedly instigated the burning of Rome, committed suicide in AD 68 on the spot where the church of Santa Maria del Popolo now stands. Nero's bones were said to rest beneath a magnificent walnut tree that grew on the site. After his death, the emperor's malefic ghost and attendant evil spirits reportedly haunted the tomb's environs and tormented any citizens who happened to wander by.

The situation grew so disturbing that in 1099 the people requested the help of Pope Paschal II. In response, he prescribed three days of prayer and fasting. During that time, so it is said, the Virgin Mary appeared to him and directed that on the third Sunday after the fasting period, the pope was to cut down the walnut tree and unearth Nero's bones. Then, she said, both tree and bones were to be burned and the ashes thrown into the Tiber River. The pope followed the Virgin's instructions, and afterward Nero's ghost and its company of malevolent imps troubled the area no further.

Soon after the exorcism, by popular request, a chapel was built where the walnut tree had stood. In 1472, Pope Sixtus V replaced the little church with Santa Maria del Popolo, a majestic edifice that was later modified by the great sculptor and architect Giovanni Lorenzo Bernini. Bas-reliefs on the basilica's ceiling commemorate the conquest of the wicked ghost of Nero.

Three gilded bas-reliefs on the ceiling in Santa Maria del Popolo's basilica tell the legend of the church's founding: In the first (top), fiends infest a walnut tree that stands atop Nero's bones. Some of the evil spirits are attacking a passer-by. Next, Pope Paschal II is visited by the Virgin Mary (center), who explains how to banish Nero's ghost. In the final relief, the pope takes an ax to the tree while Mary and Jesus look on.

really wonder if they have just been footling around and getting nowhere." She had a point: The case histories of psychic events rarely come to tidy endings—witness Garrett's own experience at Jamaica's Rose Hall, once called the most haunted house in the Western Hemisphere.

By 1952, when Garrett and a group of friends took a winter vacation in Jamaica, Rose Hall lay in ruins. But its malevolent reputation still flourished, undiminished by time. Looming high on a hill near the azure expanse of Montego Bay, the eighteenth-century manor house had passed by inheritance to one John Rose Palmer in 1818, and it was there that he brought his eighteen-year-old bride, Annie, in 1820. She was half-English and half-Irish, and the legend goes, a dark and breathtaking beauty. But their marriage was not the stuff of idyllic island romance. John, it seems, was a drunken bully. And Annie was wild and promiscuous, deeply flawed by a cruel streak that grew more pronounced with the passage of time. It was said that she practiced the dark magic of voodoo, taught her by a native priestess in Haiti, where Annie had spent her childhood.

According to local lore, the young mistress of Rose Hall took a handsome slave as her lover. When John confronted her about the liaison, she poisoned him. As he lay dying in agony, she taunted him with her infidelity and ordered her paramour to hasten her husband's demise by smothering him with a pillow. With John quite thoroughly dead, the murderers hid his corpse—most effectively, it seems, since it has never been found. Some time after the killing, Annie removed its only witness by having her lover whipped to death by other slaves.

Thereafter, Annie Palmer ruled the estate with a savage hand. Two more husbands came and went—done away with, it was said, by the mistress of Rose Hall. But husbands apparently proved an insufficient outlet for Annie's cruelty. She was fond of rakehell nocturnal horseback rides around her vast plantation. During these excursions, dressed like a man and wielding a whip, she mercilessly lashed any slave who had dared venture outside after dark.

Naturally, the slaves both hated and feared their mistress, and Annie's personal maid apparently attempted to poison her. After the girl had been convicted and executed, Annie demanded that authorities turn over to her the servant's severed head. Still dripping blood, it was borne in a basket to Rose Hall, where, atop a tapered bamboo stave, it rotted away until nothing was left but a skull gleaming white beneath the hot Jamaican sun.

In 1833, Annie Palmer was murdered, apparently by her latest lover, who may well have been taking preemptive action against his own violent demise. At any rate, household slaves found her strangled, mutilated body in her bedroom. They set fire to her bed, and later they refused to dig her grave. Finally, white neighbors ordered their own servants to bury the woman, not in the regular Saint James Parish cemetery, but beneath two feet of solid masonry in the Rose Hall garden. Her peers seemed to think that Annie had no place in hallowed ground and that mortar might discourage her evil nature from surviving her death. With its hellish mistress gone, Rose Hall gradually fell into decay. But inhabitants of the area swore that her spirit still stalked the ruins that it now shared with bats, owls, and spiders.

For Eileen Garrett, the legend of Rose Hall was an enticing lure. And although the medium visited the plantation as a tourist and not as a psychic or a psychical investigator, the trip had certain repercussions. "Even before entering the house, I was overwhelmed by clairvoyant impressions," Garrett wrote later. At her side, her secretary took notes while the medium described the images that were flooding her mind. She spoke of a woman who "is not at all as attractive as reported. She looks to me to be in her late forties. . . . One gets the impression of black hair and very flashing, stimulating blue eyes. . . . Her first husband was strange, sadistic, angry, cruel. . . . She implies that she paid too dearly for this spot that was hers. . . . She comes back so that no one can live here. She has no repentance."

Their appetites whetted by Garrett's apparent clairvoyant contact with Annie, the medium and her friends returned to Rose Hall the next night. As they emerged from a tunnel that ran beneath the ruins, Garrett walked faster and faster, then fell moaning to the ground and seemed to go into another trance. Speaking in a female voice quite different from her own, she begged, "Please, please, please." Seeking to give comfort, a member of the group said, "In God's name, you have nothing to fear." There was no coherent reply. Instead, Garrett—or was it Annie Palmer?—rolled on the ground, groaned, laughed, and sang, and pleaded with the group to pray for her.

Garrett went back twice more to Rose Hall. Once, during a seemingly clairvoyant episode, she saw Annie Palmer dying "in the night, slowly, painfully. Then I see a kind of gray light. Maybe it is the morning light. And I see someone who must have had a bad conscience gathering her up." Then, through Garrett, Annie's purported spirit made an awful vow: "Let no one think that this is the end of me. . . . My shrieks will live and those that would seek to inherit will find a curse upon them." And that was all. Despite her malediction, Annie's ghost was seen no more after Eileen Garrett's visit. Did the medium "lay the ghost?" Was there any ghost? No proof exists one way or the other, but it is said that Rose Hall grew tranquil as whatever spirits walked there faded into memory. No longer fearsome, Annie Palmer's old home has been fully and beautifully restored.

Eileen Garrett was but one of several mediums used, in effect, as laboratory guinea pigs during the years when Duke University's Joseph Rhine dominated the field of psychic research. Under his aegis, they and others labored to influence the roll of dice or identify symbols on cards withheld from their view. To the true ghost hunter, however, such endeavors were a sterile exercise. By the 1960s, investigators were taking the techniques they had learned in the laboratory and moving back into fieldwork—trying to catch ghosts where they lived, as it were, rather than piecing the facts together based on empirical experiments alone. The investigators were armed with a new technological arsenal, including such things as thermistors, which measure minute changes in temperature, microphones that can de-

tect sounds outside the range of the human ear, and even equipment that can record imperceptible changes in movements and odors. They also used what they had learned about nontechnological sensors—animals, for instance.

It has long been thought that some animals are especially sensitive to paranormal presences—a proposition that has undergone laboratory tests. In 1972, Robert Morris of the Psychical Research Foundation in Durham, North Carolina, reported on the findings of an unidentified investigator who had tested the theory on a haunted house.

Having heard of a Kentucky home in which two rooms were supposedly haunted, the investigator went to the scene, taking with him a dog, a cat, a rattlesnake, and a rat. When the dog was led into a haunted room, it instantly snarled and backed out. When the cat was carried in, it leaped onto its owner's shoulder and then to the ground, where it stood hissing, spitting, and staring at an unoccupied chair. As for the rattlesnake, it "immediately assumed an attack posture focusing on the same chair that had been of interest to the cat," Morris said. Only the rat showed no reaction whatever. When taken into another room, which had no history of haunting, all the animals behaved normally.

Among the pioneers in the use of scholarly methods in field investigations was Gertrude R. Schmeidler. In 1966, when she was a psychology professor at the City College of New York, Schmeidler took up her most famous case, that of a friend who said her home was haunted. The woman and her two adolescent children had all reported feeling the presence of an invisible ghost, which they sensed was that of a meek, anxious man.

Schmeidler dispatched an architect to make detailed floor plans of the house. The drawings were divided into a grid of more than 300 sectors, and the percipients were asked to make x's at the spots where they had received their strongest impressions of the spirit. Next, nine psychics were given the floor plans—without the x's—and asked to wander about the house, marking down their own impressions of where the ghost might be. They were also supplied with a

The ruins of Rose Hall rise against the Jamaican sky in this 1961 photograph of the

plantation house long thought to be haunted. The mansion has since been restored.

list of adjectives; some fitted the family's description of the phantom, but most did not.

After touring the house, two of the nine psychics agreed with the locations cited by the family. Interestingly, several of them also felt the strange presence in the basement, which the family had left unmarked on the grid. Four of the psychics circled the same adjectives—*meek* and *anxious*—used by the family to describe the spirit.

These results, said Schmeidler, showed "a high rate of statistical significance." Still, she concluded her report on a note of caution: "The question of what the family and the sensitives were responding to," she said, "is still open."

In 1973, one of Schmeidler's graduate students, Michaeleen Maher, used a similar technique with four psychics to investigate a New York apartment where a friend and her mother had both seen the ghost of "a hunched-over figure in a black robe." Maher reported that two psychics produced statistically significant impressions. In addition, a frame in a roll of infrared film used in the investigation showed an inexplicable "parabola of fog" in a hall supposedly frequented by the ghost. And in a pantry where one of the psychics believed the ghost was present, a Geiger counter began clicking crazily.

In all, the results were sufficiently tantalizing to persuade Maher to continue her ghost research, even while working as a research editor at *New York Magazine*. By the late 1980s, she was experimenting with a device devised by a colleague and informally labeled the Demon Detector. A kind of random number generator, the detector is a computerized device that is programmed to find anomalous light and sound in areas where unusual phenomena have been reported. Maher and her associates hope the Demon Detector might eventually be used by discarnate entities as a communications channel to the living.

It is in the use of such high-technology equipment that most investigators believe the future of psychic research to rest. Yet even as they savor such prospects, it is clear their interest lies primarily in the acquisition of information about paranormal phenomena—not in the expulsion of ghosts, a chancy task generally relegated to those who, though far less knowledgeable about psychic events, are deeply concerned with affairs of the spirit.

The Roman Catholic church, the most widely recognized authority on the rituals of exorcism, makes a distinction between ghosts—spirits of the dead—and demons, which are minions of the devil. And although the Church has elaborate rites for exorcising demons from both individuals and dwellings, it gives run-of-the-mill ghosts short shrift. The late Herbert Thurston, a Jesuit scholar of paranormal events, once remarked, "It would seem that the Catholic Church . . . has never taken very much account of those spectral appearances—ghosts in fact—that are said at times to disturb the peace of some ordinary dwelling house." It was long believed, in fact, that the Church had no exorcism ritual for the expulsion of ghosts. But Father Thurston came upon a rite that seemed, at least, pertinent to that purpose, provided the ghosts in question had evil intent. As Thurston put it, he "chanced to stumble upon a document contained in the Appendix to an edition of the *Rituale Romanum,* published with the full authorization of the Council of the Inquisition, at the royal printing office, Madrid, in the year 1631." In the newly discovered rite, the crucial conjuration said: "Do Thou, O Lord, enter graciously into the home that belongs to Thee; construct for Thyself an abiding resting-place in the hearts of Thy faithful servants, and grant that in this house no wickedness or malicious spirits may ever hold sway."

In presenting his find, Thurston expressed the hope that "this conjuration formula might . . . possibly be of service to others who found themselves in difficulty." That hope apparently remains unfulfilled, since there is no record of the ritual's ever having been used.

Despite the doctrinal standoffishness of the Catholic church, clerics still have been called on to rid a home of ghosts or poltergeists. Results vary. At Ballechin House, for example, Father Hayden tried to oust the ghost with holy water and prayers, to no avail. Clerical efforts even extended to the summoning of an archbishop to cleanse the house of its infesting spirit, but that effort also failed.

On the other hand, some ecclesiastical exorcisms of ghosts seem to have come to happier conclusions. One of the earliest cases recorded in official archives occurred in 1323 when Pope John XXII instructed John Goby, prior of Alais in Provence, to look into a haunting. It appears that a man named Guy de Torno had died eight days previously in his Alais home and that, after his death, his survivors heard his voice several times. With more than 100 laymen and three other Benedictine brothers in tow, Goby arrived at the de Torno house on Christmas Day. Although he had much more manpower than any modern investigator could hope to muster, Goby's techniques bore a striking resemblance to those that have been used ever since. His first step was to seek evidence of fraud or collusion: Not only did he station guards on the roof and rafters of de Torno's home, but he assigned others to evacuate all nearby houses and search them from top to bottom.

Taking up their nighttime vigil, Prior John and his fellow monks recited the Office for the Dead, then fell into tense silence. It was punctured by a peculiar noise, as if someone were sweeping with a broom. The presence was asked if it were that of Guy de Torno, whereupon, according to church record, a frail voice replied: "Yes, I am he."

During the conversation that followed, the voice insisted it was a "good spirit," although it had been consigned to a ghostly existence because of marital sins de Torno had committed in life. Then, with a waft of wind, the purported shade departed. Local gossip later had it returning as a dove, but Prior John and his papal master were apparently satisfied that the ghost had been laid to rest.

Unfortunately, such certitude is rare, more a product of personal experience and faith than of experiment and proof. Despite the best efforts of ghost hunters, a solution to the age-old mystery of whether some human essence survives death to haunt the living seems as remote as ever.

ACKNOWLEDGMENTS

The editors wish to thank the following individuals and institutions for their valuable assistance in the preparation of this volume:

Professor German de Argumosa, Madrid, Spain; Professor Hans Bender, Institut für Grenzgebiete der Psychologie und Psychohygiene, Freiburg, West Germany; Massimo Biondi, Rome; Manfred Böckl, Lappersdorf, West Germany; Cecelia Tabois Bonhomme, Fairfax, Va.; Dr. Adolf J. Eichenseer, Bezirksheimatpfleger Oberpfalz, Regensburg, West Germany; Alexander Ernst, Institut für Grenzgebiete der Psychologie und Psychohygiene, Freiburg, West Germany; Hilary Evans, London; Dr. Sigfrid Färber, Barbing-Eltheim, West Germany; Leif Geiges, Staufen, West Germany; Dr. Elmar Gruber, Bretten, West Germany; Ho Wen-Hui, Lecturer of the Chinese University of Hong Kong, Hong Kong; Peter Kempf, Chief Librarian, Fürstlich Hohenzollernsche Hofkammer, Sigmaringen, West Germany; Nick Clark Lowes, London; Eleanor O'Keeffe, London; Miguel Rodriguez, Jaen, Spain; Padre Umberto Scipioni, Rome; Dr. Rolf Streichardt, Institut für Grenzgebiete der Psychologie und Psychohygiene, Freiburg, West Germany; Giorgio Harold Stuart, Montepulciano, Italy; Alan Wesencraft, Harry Price Library, University of London, London.

BIBLIOGRAPHY

Alexander, John, *Ghosts: Washington's Most Famous Ghost Stories*. Washington, D.C.: Washingtonian Books, 1975.

Alexander, Marc, *Haunted Castles*. London: Frederick Muller, 1974.

Alvarado, Carlos S.:
  "Paranormal Faces: The Bélmez Case." *Theta*, summer 1983.
  "Poltergeist Research and Conceptualizations in the United States." *Theta*, spring 1983.

Angoff, Allan, *Eileen Garrett and the World beyond the Senses*. New York: William Morrow, 1974.

Baird, A. T., ed., *One Hundred Cases for Survival after Death*. New York: Bernard Ackerman, 1944.

Baker, Margaret, *Folklore of the Sea*. North Pomfret, Vt.: David & Charles, 1979.

Bardens, Dennis, *Ghosts and Hauntings*. New York: Taplinger, 1968.

Bassett, Wilbur, *Wander-Ships: Folk-Stories of the Sea*. Chicago: Open Court, 1917.

Bayless, Raymond:
  "An Electronic 'Poltergeist'?" *Theta*, summer 1980.
  The Enigma of the Poltergeist. West Nyack, N.Y.: Parker, 1967.

Beale, Marie, *Decatur House and Its Inhabitants*. Washington, D.C.: National Trust for Historic Preservation, 1954.

Betty, L. Stafford, "Kern City Poltergeist: A Case Severely Straining the Living Agent Hypothesis." *Journal of the Society for Psychical Research*, October 1984.

Brown, Raymond Lamont:
  A Casebook of Military Mystery. Cambridge, England: Patrick Stephens, 1974.
  Phantoms of the Sea: Legends, Customs and Superstitions. New York: Taplinger, 1972.

Bunch, Kyle J., and Michael K. White, "The Riddle of the Colorado Ghost Lights." *Skeptical Inquirer*, spring 1988.

Cameron, Teresa, and William G. Roll, "An Investigation of Apparitional Experiences." *Theta*, winter 1983.

Carrington, Hereward, *True Ghost Stories*. New York: J. S. Ogilvie, 1915.

Carrington, Hereward, and Nandor Fodor, *Haunted People*. New York: E. P. Dutton, 1951.

Cochran, Tracy, "The Real Ghostbusters." *Omni*, August 1988.

Compton, Piers, *The Story of Bisham Abbey*. London: Thames Valley Press, 1973.

Cornell, A. D., "Further Experiments in Apparitional Observation." *Journal of the Society for Psychical Research*, December 1960.

Cornell, A. D., and Alan Gauld, "A 'Ghost' on Television." *Journal of the Society for Psychical Research*, Vol. 45, Issue 739.

De Leau, Esther, "An Unusual and Recurrent Experience." *Journal of the American Society for Psychical Research*, October 1951.

Dingwall, E. J., K. M. Goldney, and T. H. Hall, "Mr. Hastings and the Borley Report." *Journal of the Society for Psychical Research*, June 1969.

Dingwall, Eric J., and Trevor H. Hall, *Four Modern Ghosts*. London: Gerald Duckworth, 1958.

Ebon, Martin, ed., *True Experiences with Ghosts*. New York: New American Library, 1968.

Eddington, Alexander, *Castles and Historic Homes of the Border*. Edinburgh: Oliver and Boyd, 1949.

Edinburgh Psychic College, "Penkaet Castle." *Journal of the American Society for Psychical Research*, October 1947.

Evans, Joan, "An End to *An Adventure*." *Encounter*, October 1976.

Farson, Daniel, *The Hamlyn Book of Ghosts in Fact and Fiction*. London: Hamlyn, 1978.

Finucane, R. C., *Appearances of the Dead: A Cultural History of Ghosts*. Buffalo, N.Y.: Prometheus Books, 1984.

"Fish and Men in the Maine Islands." *Harper's New Monthly Magazine*, September 1880.

Flammarion, Camille, *Haunted Houses*. Detroit: Tower Books, 1971 (reprint of 1924 edition).

Fodor, Nandor, *The Haunted Mind: A Psychoanalyst Looks at the Supernatural*. New York: Helix Press, 1960.

Forbes, William, *Hermitage Castle: Its Ruins and Historical and Traditional Associations*. Hawick, England: W. & J. Kennedy, 1839.

Forman, Joan:
  "A Stroll into the Past." *The Unexplained* (London), Vol. 4, Issue 45.
  "When Time Slips." *The Unexplained* (London), Vol. 3, Issue 33.

Fraser, Antonia, *Mary Queen of Scots*. New York: Delacorte Press, 1969.

Friedrich, Otto, *Clover*. New York: Simon and Schuster, 1979.

Garrett, Eileen, *Many Voices: The Autobiography of a Medium*. New York: G. P. Putnam's Sons, 1968.

Gauld, Alan, "The Hauntings of Abbey House, Cambridge." *Journal of the Society for Psychical Research*, September 1972.

Gauld, Alan, and A. D. Cornell, *Poltergeists*. London: Routledge & Kegan Paul, 1979.

Gold, Peter, "Tibetan Ghost Exorcism Ceremony: Images and Captions" (essay and slides). Peter Gold, © 1988.

Goode, James M., *The Outdoor Sculpture of Washington, D.C.* Washington, D.C.: Smithsonian Institution Press, 1974.

Gruber, Elmar R., "Four German Poltergeists." *Theta*, winter 1980.

Gurney, Gene, *Beautiful Washington, D.C.: A Picture Story of the Nation's Capital*. New York: Crown, 1969.

Haining, Peter, *Ghosts*. London: Book Club Associates, 1974.

Hall, Trevor H.:
  New Light on Old Ghosts. London: Duckworth, 1965.
  The Strange Story of Ada Goodrich Freer. London: Duckworth, 1968.

Hart, Hornell, "Six Theories about Apparitions." *Proceedings of the Society for Psychical Research*, May 1956.

Hastings, Arthur C., "The Oakland Poltergeist." *Journal of the American Society for Psychical Research*, July 1978.

Hastings, Robert J., "An Examination of the Dieppe Raid Case." *Journal of the Society for Psychical Research*, June 1969.

Haynes, Renée, *The Society for Psychical Research 1882-1982: A History*. London: MacDonald, 1982.

Hibbert, Samuel, *Sketches of the Philosophy of Apparitions*. New York: Arno Press, 1975.

Hole, Christina, *Haunted England: A Survey of English Ghost-Lore*. New York: Scribner's, 1941.

Holms, A. Campbell, *The Facts of Psychic Science and Philosophy: Collated and Discussed*. New Hyde Park, N.Y.: University Books, 1969.

Holzer, Hans:
  Ghosts I've Met. Indianapolis: Bobbs-Merrill, 1965.
  The Ghosts That Walk in Washington. Garden City, N.Y.:

Doubleday, 1971.
The Great British Ghost Hunt. Indianapolis: Bobbs-Merrill, 1975.
Hans Holzer's Haunted Houses. New York: Crown, 1971.
Hope, Lord Charles, and Mrs. Frank Heywood, "Report of a Visit to Brook House, Frimley." *Journal of the Society for Psychical Research,* May-June 1949.
Hopkins, R. Thurston, *Ghosts over England.* London: Meridian Books, 1952 (reprint of 1915 edition).
Huby, Pamela M., "New Evidence about 'Rose Morton.'" *Journal of the Society for Psychical Research,* December 1970.
Huggett, Richard, *Supernatural on Stage: Ghosts and Superstitions of the Theatre.* New York: Taplinger, 1975.
Huisman, Philippe, and Marguerite Jallut, *Marie Antoinette.* London: Patrick Stephens with Edita Lausanne, 1970.
Hyams, Joe, "Haunted." *The Saturday Evening Post,* July 2, 1966.
Ingram, John H., *The Haunted Homes and Family Traditions of Great Britain.* London: Gibbings, 1901.
Iremonger, L., *The Ghosts of Versailles: A Critical Study.* London: Faber, 1957.
Kemp, Gérald Van der, *Versailles.* New York: Vendome Press, 1978.
Kurtz, Paul, "A Case Study of the West Pittston 'Haunted' House." *Skeptical Inquirer,* winter 1986-1987.
Kurtz, Paul, ed., *A Skeptic's Handbook of Parapsychology.* Buffalo, N.Y.: Prometheus Books, 1985.
Lamb, C., Alan Gauld, and A. D. Cornell, "An East Midlands Poltergeist." Parts 1 and 2. *Journal of the Society for Psychical Research,* March 1973.
Lambert, G. W.:
"Antoine Richard's Garden: A Postscript to 'An Adventure.'" Parts 1 and 2. Journal of the Society for Psychical Research, July-October 1953.
"Antoine Richard's Garden: A Postscript to 'An Adventure.'" Part 3. *Journal of the Society for Psychical Research,* March 1954.
"Antoine Richard's Garden: A Postscript to 'An Adventure': A Supplementary Note." *Journal of the Society for Psychical Research,* March 1955.
"Antoine Richard's Garden: Some Further Notes." *Journal of the Society for Psychical Research,* Vol. 38, Issue 699.
"Beavor Lodge: An Old Ghost Story Retold." *Journal of the Society for Psychical Research,* June 1964.
"The Geography of London Ghosts." *Journal of the Society for Psychical Research,* December 1960.
"Phantom Scenery." *Journal of the Society for Psychical Research,* Vol. 42, Issue 721.
Lambert, G. W., and Kathleen Gay, "The Dieppe Raid Case: A Collective Auditory Hallucination." *Journal of the Society for Psychical Research,* June 1952.
Lawden, D. F., "On a Poltergeist Case." *Journal of the Society for Psychical Research,* June 1979.
Leish, Kenneth W., and the Editors of the Newsweek Book Division, *The White House.* New York: Newsweek, 1972.
Lindsay, Maurice, *The Castles of Scotland.* London: Constable, 1986.

Lisser, Herbert G. de, *The White Witch of Rosehall.* Kingston, Jamaica: Macmillan Caribbean, 1982 (reprint of 1929 edition).
McArthur, Margaret, *Scottish Ghosts.* London: James Pike, 1975.
McClenon, James, "A Summary of an Investigation of a Haunting in Baltimore." *Theta,* autumn 1981.
McEwan, P. J. M., "The Ardachie Case." *Journal of the Society for Psychical Research,* December 1955.
McHarg, James F., "A Vision of the Aftermath of the Battle of Nechtanesmere AD 685." *Journal of the Society for Psychical Research,* December 1978.
MacKenzie, Andrew:
Apparitions and Ghosts: A Modern Study. London: Arthur Barker, 1971.
"A Case of Haunting in Kent." *Journal of the Society for Psychical Research,* September 1967.
A Gallery of Ghosts: An Anthology of Reported Experience. New York: Taplinger, 1972.
Hauntings and Apparitions. London: Granada, 1983.
The Seen and the Unseen. London: Weidenfeld & Nicolson, 1987.
The Unexplained: Some Strange Cases in Psychical Research. London: Arthur Barker, 1966.
Macnaghten, Angus, *Haunted Berkshire.* Newbury, Berkshire, England: Countryside Books, 1986.
Maddocks, Melvin, and the Editors of Time-Life Books, *The Great Liners* (The Seafarers series). Alexandria, Va.: Time-Life Books, 1978.
Marsden, Simon, *The Haunted Realm: Ghosts, Spirits and Their Uncanny Abodes.* New York: E. P. Dutton, 1986.
"Medium Lays a Tudor Ghost." *News Chronicle* (London), October 30, 1936.
Miller, F. C., "Mr. Miller's Statement." Letter to Maude Ffoulkes dated July 19, 1936. Society for Psychical Research, London (unpublished).
Moberly, C. A. E., and E. F. Jourdain, *An Adventure.* Ed. by Joan Evans. London: Faber and Faber, 1911.
Morton, James, *The Poetical Remains of the Late Dr. John Leyden with Memoirs of His Life.* London: Longman, Hurst, Rees, Orme, and Brown, 1819.
Myers, Arthur, *The Ghostly Register.* Chicago: Contemporary Books, 1986.
Nisbet, Brian C.:
"On Some Enquiries Answered on Behalf of the SPR during 1978." *Journal of the Society for Psychical Research,* June 1979.
"A West Croydon 'Poltergeist.'" *Journal of the Society for Psychical Research,* December 1979.
Osis, Karlis, and Donna McCormick, "A Poltergeist Case without an Identifiable Living Agent." *Journal of the American Society for Psychical Research,* January 1982.
Owen, A. R. G., *Can We Explain the Poltergeist?* New York: Garrett, 1964.
Owen, Iris M., and Paulene Mitchell, "The Alleged Haunting of Borley Rectory." *Journal of the Society for Psychical Research,* September 1979.
Parks, Lillian Rogers, with Frances Spatz Leighton, *My Thirty Years Backstairs at the White House.* New York: Fleet, 1961.

Parrott, Ian, *The Music of 'An Adventure.'* London: Regency Press, 1966.
Parsons, Coleman O., *Witchcraft and Demonology in Scott's Fiction.* Edinburgh: Oliver & Boyd, 1964.
Parsons, Denys, "A Non-Existent Building Located." *Journal of the Society for Psychical Research,* Vol. 41, Issue 712.
Permutt, Cyril, *Beyond the Spectrum: A Survey of Supernormal Photography.* Cambridge, England: Patrick Stephens, 1983.
Persinger, Michael A., and Robert A. Cameron, "Are Earth Faults at Fault in Some Poltergeist-Like Episodes?" *Journal of the American Society for Psychical Research,* January 1986.
"Poltergeists Are Not to Blame, He Says." *Belfast Telegraph* (Northern Ireland), June 10, 1955.
Price, H. H., "Haunting and the 'Psychic Ether' Hypothesis." *Proceedings of the Society for Psychical Research,* Part 160, 1939.
Price, Harry, *Poltergeist over England: Three Centuries of Mischievous Ghosts.* London: Country Life, 1945.
Randi, James, "The Columbus Poltergeist Case: Part 1." *Skeptical Inquirer,* spring 1985.
Rogo, D. Scott:
An Experience of Phantoms. New York: Taplinger, 1974.
The Haunted House Handbook. New York: Grosset & Dunlap, 1978.
"The Poltergeist and Family Dynamics: A Report on a Recent Investigation." *Journal of the Society for Psychical Research,* February 1982.
The Poltergeist Experience. Harmondsworth, Middlesex, England: Penguin Books, 1979.
"A Poltergeist in Los Angeles." *Theta,* fall 1980.
Roll, William G.:
The Poltergeist. Metuchen, N.J.: Scarecrow Press, 1976.
"Queen Mary Investigation: Preliminary Report." Carrollton, Ga.: West Georgia College and Psychical Research Foundation, no date.
Roll, William G., ed., *Research in Parapsychology 1978.* Metuchen, N.J.: Scarecrow Press, 1979.
Roll, William G., John Beloff, and Reah A. White, eds., *Research in Parapsychology 1982.* Metuchen, N.J.: Scarecrow Press, 1983.
Rose Hall. St. James Parish, Jamaica: Rose Hall Ltd., 1973.
Roy, Archie, "Living in the Past." *The Unexplained* (London), Vol. 8, Issue 86.
Russell, Eric, *Ghosts.* London: B. T. Batsford, 1970.
Sabine, W. H. W., "Is There a Case for Retrocognition?" *Journal of the American Society for Psychical Research,* April 1950.
Salter, W. H., *Ghosts and Apparitions.* London: G. Bell, 1938.
Scott, Sir Walter, *The Bride of Lammermoor.* London: J. M. Dent, 1957 (reprint of 1907 edition).
Sergeant, Philip W., *Historic British Ghosts.* London: Hutchinson, 1936.
Shaeffer, Robert, "The Haunting of the Ivan Vassilli." *Skeptical Inquirer,* winter 1983-1984.
Shay, Frank, *A Sailor's Treasury.* New York: W. W. Norton, 1951.
Shepard, Leslie A., ed., *Encyclopedia of Occultism and Para-*

psychology. Vol. 2. Detroit, Mich.: Gale Research, 1984.

Shore, Joseph, and John Stewart, *In Old St. James: A Book of Parish Chronicles.* Kingston, Jamaica: Aston W. Gardner, 1911.

Sitwell, Sacheverell, *Poltergeists.* New York: University Books, 1959.

Smith, Susy:
Ghosts around the House. New York: World, 1970.
Haunted Houses for the Millions. New York: Dell, 1967.
Prominent American Ghosts. Cleveland, Ohio: World, 1967.

Smyth, Frank, "The Bell Witch Strikes." *The Unexplained,* Vol. 9, Issue 103.

Stevenson, Ian, "Are Poltergeists Living or Are They Dead?" *Journal of the American Society for Psychical Research,* July 1972.

Stirling, A. M. W., *Ghosts Vivisected.* New York: Citadel, 1958.

"The Story of the Winchester House." Fact sheet from the Winchester Mystery House Gardens and Museum, San Jose, Calif., 1985.

Sturge-Whiting, J. R., *The Mystery of Versailles: A Complete Solution.* London: Rider, 1937.

Tabori, Paul, *Harry Price: The Biography of a Ghost-Hunter.* London: Athenaeum Press, 1950.

Thurston, Herbert, *Ghosts and Poltergeists.* Ed. by J. H. Crehan. London: Burns, Oates and Washbourne, 1953.

Tringale, Steven V., "Two RSPK Cases in New England." *Theta,* fall 1980.

Turner, K. H., "A South Yorkshire Haunt." *Journal of the Society for Psychical Research,* September 1970.

Tyrrell, G. N. M.:
Apparitions. London: Duckworth, 1953.
"Case: Haunted House." *Journal of the Society for Psychical Research,* November-December 1943.

Underwood, Peter:
A Gazetteer of British, Scottish and Irish Ghosts. New York: Bell, 1973.

The Ghost Hunters. London: Robert Hale, 1985.

Villiers, Alan, *Men, Ships and the Sea.* Washington, D.C.: National Geographic Society, 1973.

Wainwright, F. T., "Nechtanesmere." *Antiquity,* June 1948.

West, D. J.:
"The 'Haunted' Dance Hall." *Journal of the Society for Psychical Research,* October-November 1948.
"Recent Cases of Haunting." *Journal of the Society for Psychical Research,* December 1947.

White, Rhea A., *Surveys in Parapsychology: Reviews of the Literature, with Updated Bibliographies.* Metuchen, N.J.: Scarecrow Press, 1976.

Wilson, Colin, *Poltergeist! A Study in Destructive Haunting.* London: Hodder and Stoughton, 1981.

Woelfl, Genevieve, *Psychic Experience: An Introduction to Spiritualism.* Menlo Park, Calif.: Redwood, no date.

Zorab, George, and Andrew MacKenzie, "A Modern Haunting." *Journal of the Society for Psychical Research,* March 1980.

PICTURE CREDITS

The sources for the illustrations in this book are listed below. Credits from left to right are separated by semicolons; credits from top to bottom are separated by dashes.

Country Life, London, detail from pages 12, 13. 8, 9: Crown Copyright: Royal Commission on Ancient Monuments, Scotland. 10, 11: Simon Marsden, London. 12, 13: *Country Life,* London. 14, 15: Alex Eberl, Regensburg, West Germany. 16, 17: Simon Marsden, London. 19: Art by Rebecca Butcher, copied by Larry Sherer. 20, 21: Allan Grant, Los Angeles. 22, 23: Art by Alfred T. Kamajian, copied by Larry Sherer. 26: Syndication International Ltd., London—Mary Evans Picture Library/Society for Psychical Research, London. 27: National Maritime Museum, Greenwich, England. 28: North Tyneside Libraries, North Shields, Tyne and Wear, England. 31: By courtesy of the Board of Trustees of the Victoria and Albert Museum (Theatre Museum), London—courtesy of the Hampden-Booth Theatre Library at The Players, New York. 32, 33: Metz, Tübingen, West Germany. 35: McEwan Gallery; Colin Godman, Bristol, England. 39: Northfield School, Watford, England; Mary Evans Picture Library/Society for Psychical Research, London. 40, 41: Background, Eugene Atget, courtesy Gilman Paper Company Collection, © ARS/SPADEM, 1989; inset, Bodleian Library, Oxford (courtesy T. M. Schuller, Oxford). 42, 43: Background, Dmitri Kessel, Paris, inset art by Wendy Popp; inset, Bodleian Library, Oxford (courtesy T. M. Schuller, Oxford). 44, 45: Background, Roger-Viollet, Paris, inset art by Wendy Popp; inset, Bodleian Library, Oxford (courtesy T. M. Schuller, Oxford). 46, 47: Inset, Bodleian Library, Oxford (courtesy T. M. Schuller, Oxford); background, Roger-Viollet, Paris, inset art by Wendy Popp. 48, 49: Inset, Bod-leian Library, Oxford (courtesy T. M. Schuller, Oxford); background, Eugene Atget/Archives Photographiques, Paris, © ARS/SPADEM, 1989, inset art by Wendy Popp. 50, 51: Adolf Ulrik Wertmüller, "Marie Antoinette," from the Nationalmuseum, Stockholm; Pascal Lemaître, Paris, Collection Archives Départementales des Yvelines. 53: Art by Rebecca Butcher, copied by Larry Sherer. 54: Mary Evans Picture Library, London. 57: Courtesy of The British Library, London. 58: Massachusetts Historical Society, Boston. 59: Mansell Collection, London; Mary Evans Picture Library, London. 60: Mary Evans Picture Library, London. 61: Mary Evans Picture Library, London—National Portrait Gallery, London. 62: Hulton Picture Library, London. 63: Guildhall Library/Bridgeman Art Library, London. 65: Harry Price Collection, University of London. 66: Harry Price Collection, University of London—Mary Evans Picture Library, London/Harry Price Collection, University of London. 67: From *Hauntings,* by Peter Underwood, J. M. Dent & Sons Ltd., London, 1977—Harry Price Collection, University of London. 68, 69: Harry Price Collection, University of London. 71: Society for Psychical Research, London. 72, 73: William George Roll, West Georgia College, Carrollton. 75: Courtesy Queen Mary Historical Archives, Long Beach, California, detail from pages 82, 83. 76, 77: Mary Evans Picture Library, London. 78, 79: From an album in George Eastman House, Rochester, New York, Smithsonian Institution Neg. No. 47629. 80, 81: *Harpers New Monthly Magazine,* September 1880, courtesy Library of Congress. 82, 83: Courtesy Queen Mary Historical Archives, Long Beach, California. 85: Art by Rebecca Butcher, copied by Larry Sherer. 87: Art by Lisa F. Semerad. 88: Andrew MacKenzie, London. 90, 91: From *Monks, Nuns and Monasteries,* by Sacheverall Sitwell, George Weidenfeld & Nicholson Ltd. Publishers, London, 1965. 94: The Bettmann Archive, New York. 95: From *An Authenticated History of the Famous Bell Witch,* by M. V. Ingram, Rare Book Reprints, Nashville, Tennessee, 1961. 96, 97: Elmar Gruber, Bretten, West Germany; Miguel Rodriguez, Belmez, Spain (3)—Institut für Grenzgebiete der Psychologie und Psychohygiene, Freiburg, West Germany. 98: Harry Price Library, University of London. 99: Art by Lisa F. Semerad. 100, 101: Raeanne Rubenstein/*PEOPLE Weekly,* © 1978 The Time Inc. Magazine Group, all rights reserved, inset Tony Korody/Sygma. 102: Art by Lisa F. Semerad. 105: Llewellyn/Uniphoto, inset map by Tina Taylor. 106, 107: Photomontage, Library of Congress; Rhoda Baer. 108, 109: Copyrighted by the White House Historical Association, photograph by The National Geographic Society; photomontage, Derry Moore, figure Library of Congress. 110, 111: Photomontage, Ping Amranand, figure courtesy Independence National Historical Park Collection, Philadelphia; Rhoda Baer from *Ghosts: Washington's Most Famous Ghost Stories,* by John Alexander, Washingtonian Books, Washington, D.C., 1976. 112, 113: Nina Leen/*LIFE Magazine,* © Time Inc.; photomontage, Ping Amranand, figure courtesy Massachusetts Historical Society, Boston. 115: Art by Rebecca Butcher, copied by Larry Sherer. 116-119: Society for Psychical Research, London. 120, 121: Courtesy Winchester Mystery House, San Jose, California. 122: Mary Evans Picture Library/Society for Psychical Research, London. 124: Society for Psychical Research, London. 125: E. Honeyman, Ballechin, Scotland. 126, 127: Peter Gold, Santa Fe. 129: Mary Evans Picture Library/Society for Psychical Research, London. 131: De Antonis, Rome, courtesy S. Maria del Popolo, Rome. 134, 135: Courtesy Rollins Jamaica Ltd., Rose Hall, Jamaica. 136, 137: Marilyn Krauss, courtesy Michaeleen Maher, New York.

INDEX

Hauntings was originally published as part
of the series:

MYSTERIES OF THE UNKNOWN

SERIES DIRECTOR: Russell B. Adams, Jr.
Series Administrator: Myrna Traylor-Herndon
Designer: Susan K. White

Editorial Staff for *Hauntings*
Associate Editors: Scarlet Cheng (pictures);
Janet Cave, Laura Foreman, Jim Hicks (text)
Researchers: Christian D. Kinney, Philip Murphy,
Sharon Obermiller
Assistant Designer: Susan M. Gibas
Copy Coordinators: Mary Beth Oelkers-Keegan,
Jarelle S. Stein
Picture Coordinator: Betty H. Weatherley
Editorial Assistant: Donna Fountain

Special Contributors: Christine Hinze (London, picture
research); Mary Ford Dreesen (lead research); Sheila
Greene, David Mitchell, Evelyn Prettyman, Jacqueline
Shaffer, Pamela L. Whitney (research); Janelle Biddinger,
Sarah Brash, Leslie Carper, Champ Clark, Lydia Preston
Hicks, Robert Kiener, John I. Merritt, Dirk Olin, Jake Page,
Charles Phillips, Charles C. Smith, Daniel Stashower (text);
John Drummond (design); Hazel Blumberg-McKee (index)

Correspondents: Elisabeth Kraemer-Singh (Bonn), Vanessa
Kramer (London), Maria Vincenza Aloisi (Paris), Ann
Natanson (Rome)
Valuable assistance was also provided by Angelika Lem-
mer (Bonn); Judy Aspinall (London); Pilar Gore (Madrid);
Elizabeth Brown, Christina Lieberman (New York); Ann
Wise (Rome).

The Consultant:
Marcello Truzzi, the general consultant for the series, is a
professor of sociology at Eastern Michigan University. He
is also director of the Center for Scientific Anomalies
Research (CSAR) and editor of its journal, the *Zetetic
Scholar.* Dr. Truzzi, who considers himself a "constructive
skeptic" with regard to claims of the paranormal, works
through the CSAR to produce dialogues between critics
and proponents of unusual scientific claims.